THE
PARABLES
of
JESUS

THE PARABLES

of

JESUS

Denis McBride C.Ss.R

A Redemptorist Publication

Published by

Redemptorist Publications

A Registered Charity Limited by guarantee. Registered in England 3261721

Cover illustration: "Female Torso", Kasimir Malevich, Superstock Ltd
Cover design: Rosemarie Pink

Denis McBride © 1999

ISBN 0 85231 192 3

First printed March 1999
Third printing November 2005

Scriptural quotations are from
the Revised Standard Version of the Bible,
copyrighted 1946, 1952, © 1971, 1973;
and from the New Revised Standard Version of the Bible,
copyright 1989 by the Division of Christian Education
of the National Council of the Churches of Christ in the USA.
All rights reserved. Used by permission.

Printed by Cambridge University Press, CB2 2BS

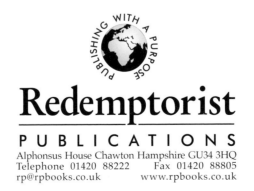

Redemptorist

P U B L I C A T I O N S
Alphonsus House Chawton Hampshire GU34 3HQ
Telephone 01420 88222   Fax 01420 88805
rp@rpbooks.co.uk   www.rpbooks.co.uk

For two Susans

in memory of
my mother, Susan,
whose imaginative sympathy
led her to populate my childhood
with people and stories that still delight

and for

Susan Ferry, my redoubtable niece,
who survived to tell the tale
and who has since thrived
in crafting a new story
of her own life

Contents

Preface

There were four of us, two girls and two boys. Throughout our childhood in Scotland our mother used to tell us stories, including tales of her own country childhood and youth in Ireland, and these last would leave us wide-eyed with jealousy because her experience of growing up seemed so much wilder than our own tame affair. Compared to the lunar calendar of her upbringing, the mix of people she knew and the adventures she had, our lives seemed to be forever stuck in what liturgists are pleased to call "ordinary time".

Listening to her, however, we found it difficult to tell from any particular story if it was true or not. Truth, for the four of us, meant that the story had to match what actually happened if it was to merit entry into the book of *true* stories. About that we were clear. We prided ourselves that we could distinguish between the world of fairy tales and the real world that we scanned in the daily news: one was imaginary, the other real. We could distinguish, after all, between "Once upon a time there was a king who had three daughters . . ." and "Yesterday in Parliament". The boundaries were well established, the limits clearly defined – that is, of course, until we listened to her.

Her stories often seemed too magical to be true, too funny or too sad to be real, too far away in a Donegal landscape of lonely hills and soft-spoken people to connect with the regular round of our life as children from a big city. Her natural sense of drama, her delight in the awkward and the eccentric, the crooked and the cracked, seemed to disqualify her as a reporter of the sheer ordinariness of life. The stories she unfolded would be populated with strange people that never seemed to fit into our simple view of the world, characters that carried ambiguity around with them as if it were a badge of honour.

There was a cranky aunt, a lover of litanies and devotions to obscure saints, who was a secret terrorist. There was an ancient uncle who sat wrapped in silence, like some displaced Buddha, moving only to stoke the turf fire – a man who had travelled the reaches of the world and whose adopted silence on his return covered over an encyclopaedia of loss. There was a doctor, living in a huge house facing out to the raging spread of the Atlantic Ocean, who had acquired a gift for cruelty. There was an old crone who lived alone, except for the company of an overdressed Infant of Prague, in a caravan without curtains. Every day the two of them looked out in stubborn hope for the return of her lost children, whose refusal to visit her was puzzling, since she appeared to be the kindliest soul to grace God's earth. And then there was the omnipresent village idiot – a small man shaped like a U-turn in reverse, whose perpetual alcoholic grin greeted you as a *Dominus vobiscum*, and who turned out to be much wiser than the parish priest.

They all tumbled out onto the story's stage, collectors' items, all of them. Where did they come from, we wondered: our mother's memory or her imagination? Or a secret alliance between both? How real were they?

None of us had come even close to developing her sense of ambiguity about the world, her acute perception about what hurt people and what haunted them, her respect for the secrets people carry and for the fictional lives they end up leading to hide them. We might have guessed that she carried her own secrets, but it was still too early. Years later, listening to President Mitterand being interviewed shortly before his death, I thought of her when Mitterand shared his favourite quotation, spoken by a Cardinal de Retz: "One abandons a sense of ambiguity at one's peril." She and de Retz, I thought, would have got along fine.

When her story was finished, the four of us would ask our earnest question, "But, Mammy, is it true?" – as if we were miniature detectives trained to respect only the bare facts. She would appear, at first, mildly hurt by such a confining question and then she would offer her predictable response – a twinkle in her eyes and a call for yet another cup of tea. About the origin of the story, we were always left no wiser than when the story started. The tea called.

When we went to Ireland, during the summer holidays, we travelled like tenderfoots into her land of story. Her magical settings became our playground, where we made new friends with donkeys and horses, fitful dogs and solemn cows, and chased the hens as if they were escaped gangsters on the run. We ran up and down lanes laden with red and purple fuschias, playing hide-and-seek behind the drooping flowers that we called Chinese bells. We played in abandoned farmhouses, whose tiny roofless rooms still harboured reluctant ghosts; along beautiful stretches of empty beach, we learned to call the strand; through tiny fields of stacked hay and over dry-stone walls into the endless emptiness of hills.

Apart from the time when the four of us played together, we went everywhere together as a family. We prayed barefoot at holy wells, murmuring rosaries as we hobbled around a makeshift shrine, then left some token – a button, a comb, a hairpin – to placate the Celtic god of place. On rainy days, which were fewer than they seemed, we visited the Singing Kettle (more tea) and sat looking out at the slow traffic of the town, as if we were watching a silent film that was struggling to introduce a plot. When we crossed the hills between my mother's home-place and my father's, we would pause by the tiny loch of Columcille and pay our respects to the runaway saint who had paused to watch the dancing fish, and then, when his pursuers caught up, cursed the loch to harbour no more life.

Of course, there was a litany of relatives to visit, a duty I confess I hated, so I would tag along behind the others as if trudging around endless stations of the cross. The relatives would always welcome us warmly, if somewhat warily – "the Scotch" they called us – and heap more cups of tea into our lap as they enquired about the lives of those who got away. For them it must have seemed that we were eager exiles returning only to reconfirm the reasons why we left. If there was any pause or awkwardness in the conversation, it was always covered by the responsorial psalm: "You'll have some tea." You could only consent.

For the summer holidays we remained afloat on a sea of tea-leaves. And everywhere we went the landscape of heather and hills and ocean opened out to us and spread its stark beauty before us; but everywhere, for me, there were too many rocks, too much wind, and too much emptiness. It was a landscape to be lonely in.

Perhaps the emptiness of the landscape enlarged the character of its inhabitants, so that eventually they measured up to their huge stage. I don't know. But I do remember we met some of her characters, and we were sometimes shocked how real her portraits proved to be when we could identify people, without her help. Delighted, she would whisper down to us: "See, now, didn't I tell you?" They were there, all right, but as I remember they appeared much smaller, somehow, than in her stories. More straightforward, less poised for anecdotal celebrity. Her tales gave them a mythic grandeur that eluded them in life. They were ordinary folk, I persuaded myself, as uncomplicated as us.

I remember that I stopped playing the detective to her stories, that I gave up asking the inane question, "Is it true?" I wish I could remember when that was or, more importantly, what led me to abandon the question. Was it because I was, at long last, catching something of her belief in the usefulness of fiction to highlight truth that could not be safely told without a little dressing? I would like to believe so, but it's far more likely that it was because I knew I would never receive her answer.

When we come to reading the parables of Jesus, there is so much that remains unanswered. The parables stand, in whatever context the evangelist puts them, as insights into Jesus' use of fiction as a favoured way of teaching.

Jesus invests so much of himself, his sense of values, his elliptical way of looking at life, his coded critique of the world he inhabits, in his fiction. His parables. It is as if he believes that fiction, rather than forthright description, is a more delicate medium for carrying the strangeness of his insights and the pattern of his contrary wisdom. While fiction manufactures a world of play and pretence, of once upon a time, within the controlled safety of that never-world it can deliver observations about the real world that ache with accuracy, that leave you somewhere between belief and dread, where you end up astonished at the story's sober insight. Fiction, yes, but life in live performance. Such are the parables.

In Arundhati Roy's story, *The God of Small Things*, she tells of a small fiction devised by small children in Kerala, India. The three children – Rahel, her twin brother Estha, and their cousin, Sophie Mol – dress up in saris and pretend they are ladies from the town of Ayemenen. Dolled up, they clump their way gracelessly to visit Velutha, an untouchable, who takes delight in welcoming them:

> He greeted them with the utmost courtesy and gave them fresh coconut water to drink. He chatted to them about the weather. The river. The fact that in his opinion coconut trees were getting shorter by the year. As were the ladies in Ayemenen. He introduced them to his surly hen. He showed them his carpentry tools, and whittled them each a little wooden spoon.
>
> It is only now, these years later, that Rahel with adult hindsight recognised the sweetness of that gesture. A grown man entertaining three racoons, treating them like real ladies. Instinctively colluding in the conspiracy of their fiction, taking care not to decimate it with adult carelessness. Or affection.
>
> It is after all so easy to shatter a story. To break a chain of thought. To ruin a fragment of a dream being carried around carefully like a piece of porcelain.
>
> To let it be, to travel with it, as Velutha did, is much the harder thing to do.[1]

Velutha does not unmake the children's story by naming it a useless fantasy. He enters their fiction, travels with their play, and conspires with them in their world of make-believe. That same delicacy and respect is required to enter the fiction of Jesus, for each parable is "a fragment of a dream" that Jesus shares. Unlike the children's fiction, a parable is no momentary game devised to pass the time, but a serious play that reflects the kind of time Jesus sees we inhabit. His fiction holds up a mirror in which we see a double reflection – what we have become and what we are called to be. His fiction holds God's dream of us.

In exploring the parables our goal is to come closer to understanding the values of Jesus. Those values are in conflict with much of what Jesus witnessed in his own time. They might also be in conflict with much of what we take for granted in our own world. The purpose of our exploration is not academic but pastoral. It is to allow the subversive voice of Jesus to be heard again; it is to be confronted by another way of looking at ourselves, others, and the world around us.

I would like to thank Rosemary Gallagher, my editor, for commissioning the book on behalf of Redemptorist Publications. I sincerely hope that her trust is rewarded. Also I would like to express my gratitude to the participants of the courses at Hawkstone Hall, who over the years have entered the House of Parable, like pilgrims chancing on an ancient shrine, and wrestled with dreams much older than their own. For their everlasting kindness and support, I am deeply grateful.

Hawkstone Hall
Shropshire

---

[1] A. Roy, *The God of Small Things* (London: Flamingo, 1998) p.190

A story

Once upon a time an ancient rabbi was asked why telling stories, rather than making statements, seemed to be a more effective way of communicating with people. He thought for a while, tilted his head sideways, then scratched his dented face. Once upon a time, he said, it happened that Truth walked down a village street as naked as the day he was born. The villagers were horrified; they ran into their houses, closed and locked their doors, and refused to have anything to do with this walking vulgarity.

As Truth left the village he thought to himself, since he had only himself to think to, why he couldn't get near other people, why they were so frightened of him. He saw Story approaching the village. Story was dressed in fine, colourful clothes. She was a sight for the eyes. Some people said that when she smiled, her face looked as if she had rented the sun.

Story greeted Truth and then, keeping custody of the eyes, enquired: "What's the matter with you? Why do you look so sad and disappointed? Tell me what's wrong."

Truth said, "Nobody wants me, nobody accepts me. When people see me coming, they run away and hide. But you are always invited into their houses. They love to sit around the fire listening to you. Why does everyone avoid me?"

"May I act out of character and be totally frank with you?" Story asked.

"Please do, I would appreciate that."

"Everyone avoids you because of your nakedness," Story said. "People today are afraid of the naked truth, so they turn away. I'm sorry, Truth, but, believe me, that's the truth. You live inside your enclosure of clarity, looking out in disapproval at the fog of humanity. You emerge to clear things up. But you have never stepped out into the real world of ambiguity, confusion, and brokenness. Life is untidy, it is arbitrary, and it is too much to stare at for long. Since Adam and Eve the human story has been one of covering up, and you walk around like some noble exception, feeling no need for anything as common as a fig leaf. Why don't you use a bit of imagination? I'll tell you what. Let me make some clothes for you and then we'll see how people respond."

Truth was reluctant to accept his new friend's advice, but he was tired of loneliness and decided to risk it. Two weeks later he dressed himself in the clothes

Story had made for him. At first he felt strange and uncomfortable, all covered up; but soon he discovered to his delight that people no longer avoided him, but opened their doors and welcomed him into their houses.

Truth and Story became firm friends. Not long after, Truth and Story married. Not too long after that, they had five children, whose unusual names are recorded as Myth, Apologue, Action, Satire, and Parable.

Statement and Story

Most ordinary conversation consists of making statements or telling stories. The majority of the stories we tell one another report things that have happened, involving particular people, specific places, and distinct events. The story focuses on the world of the *particular*, gathering individual details to give colour and shape and substance to the telling. By contrast, statements convey *general* truths about people, events, and the world; they focus on meaning. Both stories and statements convey pieces of information to people, but, for most people, the story tends to be a more powerful vehicle of communication than the statement.

<u>Statement</u>	<u>Story</u>
conveys general truth, focuses on meaning	*reports particular event*
The state of Florida periodically suffers from the menace of tornadoes.	Last week whole sections of Florida were destroyed by a tornado.
Statement *in the* Gospel of John **John came as a witness,** **as a witness to speak for the light,** **so that everyone might believe through** **him. He was not the light,** **only a witness to speak for the light.** **The Word was the true light . . .**	**Story** *in the* Gospel of Luke **In the 15th year of Tiberius** **Caesar's reign when Pontius** **Pilate was governor of Judea,** **Herod, tetrarch of Galilee...** **during the pontificate of Annas** **and Caiaphas, the word of God** **came to John the Baptist in the** **wilderness.**

The evangelist John has a preference for statements, while Luke has a preference for stories. Before you meet the particular characters of Jesus and John in the

Fourth Gospel, the evangelist has already prepared you through making statements about the relationship between them. He first declares the significance they have in his account and gives you, the reader, the distilled summary of their relationship through the medium of statements about them. Luke, on the other hand, trusts his readers to work out for themselves the relationship between these two men by reading the story he unfolds.

Since Christianity is a historical religion, the truth that it teaches can be best expressed in the form of story. In Christianity the story is first, the theological statements come later; the storytellers are there before the theologians.

Whatever claims are made about the person of Jesus, these ultimately depend on the original story of Jesus. The statements that Peter makes about Jesus to the centurion Cornelius, for example, are dependent on the story of Jesus – that is, on the particular events that happened during his public ministry: "You must have heard about the recent happenings in Judea, about Jesus of Nazareth and how he began in Galilee, after John had been preaching baptism" (Acts 10:37). Thus the recent happenings in Judea form the basis for Peter's preached story about Jesus.

Why tell stories?

We can tell stories for all sorts of reasons:

> to establish who we are and where we came from;
> to preserve our traditions, to defend our way of seeing things;
> to tell lies and hide painful truths;
> to pass the time, to entertain, to enlighten;
> to expose oppressive behaviour and hypocrisy;
> to question cherished myths, to introduce new thinking.

All tribes and all peoples have a treasure of sacred stories. In many cultures it was the storyteller who introduced people to their own identity and their own history, giving them a sense of belonging to a larger story than their own. These stories have the function of establishing a narrative beginning to creation/nation/tribe and preserving a particular way of seeing the world. The stories were told in the belief that people's identities seem largely determined by the kind of story they believe they inhabit. Without those stories there is a sense of alienation not only from what has happened before but from what is happening within. Without stories there is little opportunity to discover a way of seeing the world or a way of seeing ourselves.

The appeal to narrative as a way of understanding the world and oneself is not based simply on an interest in story nor in recognition of the story's privileged place in the Jewish and Christian traditions. As Michael Goldberg points out: "Instead, it is the much stronger view that virtually all our convictions, nonreligious as well as religious, are rooted in some narrative, and that frequently, our most serious disputes with one another reflect rival narrative accounts."[1]

A particular community's sacred stories give shape to its sense of identity; they provide a setting for belief; they give rise to convictions and claims which are later abstracted from the original narrative and placed in a dogmatic framework. A community's sacred stories, however, may provoke profound disagreement among those who do not belong to that community or among its own members who can no longer subscribe to the stories' claims. Stories told, for instance, to uphold the supremacy of a particular race or justify entitlement to a particular land are rarely tales without victims – which is why counter stories are formed to question that particular way of looking at the world.

Different kinds of stories have different purposes. Without suggesting the accompanying table covers the whole spectrum, one can see five types of story, each with a different goal.[2]

Story Types	MYTH	APOLOGUE	ACTION	SATIRE	PARABLE
The story's relationship to the world beyond the story:	_establishes_ the world by foundational stories of opposites: human/divine; life/death; male/female; good/bad. Reconciling the opposites.	_defends_ the world by persuading people of its truth; these stories attempt to reinforce people's cherished convictions.	_investigates_ the world by presenting contrasting characters about whose fates we care. Usually resolved by conclusion.	_attacks_ the world by ridiculing pretentious people and institutions; these stories attempt to expose hypocrisy.	_subverts_ the world by exposing oppression and selfishness; these stories attempt to introduce new values.
Examples	Creation stories	The Tales of Aesop	Most novels and films	Political cartoons	The Rich Man and Lazarus

Moving from myth to parable is a gradual critical movement from establishing a world view in myth, defending it in apologue, exploring it in action, attacking it in satire, to subverting it in parable. Whereas myth attempts to reassure its hearers by drawing them into a world where harmony can emerge through reconciling opposites, the parable offers no such reassurance. Myth aims at stability; parable aims at change. J.D. Crossan argues that parable is the polar opposite of myth: "It (parable) is a story deliberately calculated to show the limitations of myth, to shatter world so that its relativity becomes apparent."[3] Where myth enthrones, parable dethrones. Parable does to conventional wisdom what the *Magnificat* does to social hierarchy: it overthrows it.

This is dramatically illustrated in the parable of The Rich Man and Lazarus (Lk 16:19-31). The first part of the story shows a world of accepted social division between the rich and the destitute: a street beggar seeks food from a rich householder who feasts magnificently every day. The gulf between the two characters is not bridged by compassion. The second part of the parable shows the reversal of that social system where Lazarus is elevated to the bosom of Abraham while the rich man is condemned to torment in Hades: now the one who was rich seeks water from the one who was poor. No reconciliation, it is revealed, is possible between the reaches of this new gulf, which, unlike the previous one, cannot be crossed. The parable effectively subverts the social divisions between the clean and the unclean, the elite and the outsider. It refuses to acquiesce in the quaint belief that what is tolerable in society is eternally sanctioned by God.

None of the Gospels, however, is a collection of the parables of Jesus. The parables are contained within the larger literary form of Gospel. If the Gospels emerged from different communities, the evangelists share a similar pastoral purpose in their desire to provide a foundational document for their own communities. In their writing the evangelists seek to provide a basic narrative that accounts for the origins of the Christian movement in the person of Jesus of Nazareth, the one who is now celebrated as Lord. Given the evangelists' common purpose, it comes as no surprise that each Gospel narrative will also be apologetic in its presentation of the Christian community.

The parable, given its purpose as a literary form on the critical side of the story's relationship to the world, does not sit easily inside the larger form of Gospel, which is foundational and apologetic. This tension between Gospel and parable adds to the difficulty of interpreting the parables as examples of subversive thinking.

There is a danger that the parable ends up being treated as legitimising rather than questioning the behaviour and attitudes that provoke the telling of the story. Take, for example, the parable of The Talents, particularly the conduct of the rich landowner who throws the third servant into outer darkness because he refused to play his master's exploitative game of reaping the benefits of other people's labour and property (Mt 25:14-30). Why tell *this* story? Is the parable an apologetic for the behaviour of the rich master? Is it a denunciation of the master's exploitative habit of enriching himself by reaping what others have sown? Is the third servant's refusal and his exposure of the way his employer gets rich a brave act that embodies the values of Jesus? Is it a Gospel value to take away from people the little they have and give it to those who have plenty? Is the Gospel indistinguishable from an absolute market economy?

Perhaps the continuing challenge in teaching and preaching the parables is trying to uncover the meaning of the parable consistent with the parable's literary form – which in many cases is a story told to expose and subvert destructive behaviour that is passively accepted as normal.

Only a story

Parables, of course, are fictional stories: their claim to truth does not pretend to be based on historical reminiscence or real events. When we hear or read a story we know to be a work of fiction, our first reaction may be to think of it simply as entertainment: "Interesting, yes, but it's only a story after all." Knowing a story to be fictional might lead us to dismiss any claims the story might make on us. Some people believe that historical narrative or reportage is the only "real story" worthy of their attention.

A rabbi teacher of mine told me how he found it more difficult to tell stories to Gentiles than to Jews. When you tell a story to a Gentile, he said, you hear two recurring questions:

Is it true?

Did it really happen?

He answers the first question by saying, "Yes, it is true." And the second by saying, "No, it didn't really happen." He said that when he tells his Jewish congregation a story, their question is:

What does it mean?

Elie Wiesel eloquently makes the same point when he tells the story of meeting a rabbi friend of his grandfather's in Tel Aviv, after an interim of twenty years, and trying to explain what he is doing with his life:

> "Tell me what you are doing," the Rebbe said in a soft voice. I told him I was writing. "Is that all?" he asked in disbelief. I said yes, that's all. His expression was so reproachful that I had to elaborate and explain that some writings could sometimes, in moments of grace, attain the quality of deeds. He did not seem to understand . . .
>
> "What are you writing?" the Rebbe asked. "Stories," I said. He wanted to know what kind of stories: true stories. "About people you knew?" Yes, about people I might have known. "About things that happened?" Yes, about things that happened or could have happened. "But they did not?" No, not all of them did. In fact some were invented from almost the beginning to almost the end. The Rebbe leaned forward as if to measure me up and said with more sorrow than anger: "That means you are writing lies!" I did not answer immediately. The scolded child within me had nothing to say in his defence. Yet, I had to justify myself: "Things are not that simple, Rebbe. Some events do take place but are not true; others are – although they never occurred." [4]

Wiesel sees himself as an inheritor of a rich biblical tradition where writers have always felt free to use a variety of resources from the literary store cupboard: oral tradition, ancestral myths, legends, folk-tales, dreams, visions, tribal customs, parables, hymns, genealogies, doxologies, testimonials, prayers, etc. All these were pressed into service to communicate the truth of their message. To confine the biblical writers to answering one concern – "Just tell us what actually happened!" – would not only be anachronistic but subscribe to the curious belief that all people really need, in order to change, is accurate information. Luke caricatured this naïve belief in the parable of The Rich Man and Lazarus, when Abraham says: "If they do not listen to Moses and the prophets, neither will they be convinced even if someone rises from the dead" (Lk 16:31).

How do you challenge people to change?

Throughout the Synoptic Gospels the evangelists show us Jesus inviting his hearers to use their imagination and travel into the world of parable. Sympathetic imagination enables us as listeners or readers to cross the bridge between where we are and where others are, between the way we see things and different ways of seeing the same things. While it is difficult to recover the original historical setting that gave rise to any particular parable spoken by Jesus – many of the parables are contained within blocks of teaching by the evangelists (e.g. Mk 4:1-34; Mt 24:32 – 25:46) – the nature of the parable form will help us in our task. As J. Jeremias notes: "They (the parables) were mostly concerned with a situation of conflict – with justification, defence, attack, and even challenge. For the most part, though not exclusively, they are weapons of controversy. Every one of them calls for an answer on the spot."[5]

The parables are challenges to change. They are a way of confronting people. Through the parables the evangelists present us with a Jesus who invites his hearers to use their imagination to focus on vulnerable groups or oppressive attitudes in the hope that they will see things differently.

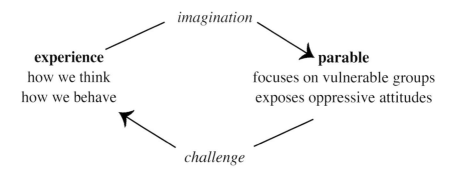

The parables' focus on vulnerable individuals or groups can be seen from the following examples:

Last Judgement	*focus >> hungry; thirsty; stranger; naked; sick; imprisoned*
Great Feast	*focus >> poor; lame; crippled; blind; people beyond our town*
Rich Man & Lazarus	*focus >> neglected beggar at the gate*
Vineyard	*focus >> unemployed who are hired last*
Talents	*focus >> 3rd slave who refuses to enrich his "hard" master*
Unforgiving Slave	*focus >> slaves who cannot pay their debts*
Lost Sheep/Coin	*focus >> the lost ones*
Father & Two Sons	*focus >> son/brother who has failed and shamed the family*
Good Samaritan	*focus >> stranger who is beaten and robbed*
Pharisee/Toll Collector	*focus >> sinner who is despised by the virtuous*
Insistent Neighbour	*focus >> host who has no food for guest*
Unjust Judge	*focus >> poor widow who is refused justice*

The focus on vulnerability concentrates the attention on how we respond to the mixture of people and situations explored. The parable provokes questions; it forces us to think about our own attitudes and behaviour; it challenges us to see the destructive and saving influence we have on one another.

The parables can be seen within the larger context of Jesus' preaching and teaching. Following John the Baptist, Jesus challenges his hearers: "Repent, for the kingdom of heaven has come near" (Mt 4:17). That call to repentance becomes the keynote of Jesus' Galilean ministry. The word repent renders the Greek *metanoiō*, which literally translates *to think across the way you normally think; to think differently; to change your mind*. The parables are at the service of that radical summons, to question what we take for granted by calling us to change our minds.

The idea of changing your mind is a much broader one than repentance, which suggests sorrow for sins and the effort to make retribution. W.H. Vanstone notes the difference in his own inimitable way:

> Repentance implies an awareness of being guilty, being ashamed of oneself and resolving to mend one's ways, but *metanoia* is much broader in its meaning. It means any kind of "change of mind"; it includes in its meaning "having second thoughts" on any matter at all and "seeing in a different light" any kind of situation. If someone who had planned to go to the bank next Monday was reminded that next Monday was a bank holiday and accordingly changed his or her plans, this would be an instance of *metanoia* – of "seeing the situation in a different light". But it would be misleading to say that the person "repented" of his or her original plan. So we must not suppose that the preachers' appeal to their hearers for *metanoia* implied that they should be ashamed of their past and resolved to mend their ways: it was rather an invitation to them to bear in mind the story they had heard and see their own situation in the light of what they had heard.[6]

Challenging people to think differently, however, is a risky pastime – not least because most of us want to be left alone to nourish our cherished prejudices. If few of us welcome criticism, fewer have a gift for offering it. How do you confront people who see things differently? How do you challenge a friend who is involved in destructive behaviour? How do you tell people things you know they do not want to hear? Answers to these questions depend largely on our cultural background and personality, but most attempts at confronting others follow either the direct approach, which concentrates on naming the problem, or the indirect approach, which has the dual focus of the problem and the relationship between the two parties.

a) ***Direct confrontation*** In this way you confront others directly by going straight to the point; you "tell it like it is". There is no attempt to disguise the issue, no striving after diplomatic language, no "beating around the bush". Your strategy is to name unambiguously what concerns you about the thinking or behaviour of the offending party. The speakers often call this "constructive criticism"; rarely is it so perceived by the listeners, who may feel affronted by what they hear. Sometimes direct confrontation accomplishes little because, no matter how accurate the criticism, it is registered by the hearers as destructive, so that they end up feeling disabled. What they hear might only serve to confirm a larger script that others have written about them: that they are born losers, that they can get nothing right, that they are chronic failures.

If the only time we relate to people is when we confront them and give them a piece of our mind, in all probability the confrontation will not have the desired result. It is difficult to challenge people profitably if there is no supporting relationship to sustain the criticism.

b) ***Indirect confrontation*** In some cultures direct confrontation is regarded as crude and harmful to relationships; instead, the confrontation is done indirectly through the medium of go-betweens or by using indirect language. This method tries to avoid anything that looks like antagonism, using coded language that needs interpretation. Although the indirect method seeks to face the issue, there is the added focus on the relationship between the parties. The reason the confrontation is managed indirectly is because of the underlying concern that the relationship should not be irreparably damaged in the process of "telling the truth".

Diplomatic language is an obvious example of this process. When the British Foreign Secretary met with his Iraqi opposite number before the Gulf War, he emerged from a meeting that had manifestly failed to reach any agreement and declared: "I am not sure I can entirely subscribe to the position adopted by Mr Aziz." The waiting journalists had no need of a code book to interpret the message. Since both parties wanted the talks to continue, they were careful about avoiding the robust language of confrontation lest that might preclude negotiations leading to agreement. In this instance, however, it did not work.

The parable as indirect confrontation

One way of responding to the question, "Why speak in parables?" is to answer that speaking in parables is a stylised way of confronting people indirectly. While there is a litany of examples in the Gospels of Jesus confronting his opponents openly, with no rumour of subtlety in the exchanges, there are as many examples of Jesus using short narrative fiction to oppose destructive attitudes and behaviour and propose radical alternatives. In these instances the parable deliberately uses the medium of fiction to encode whatever conflict is happening between Jesus and the other party. The telling of the parable permits another view to be advanced, another way to be explored.

When you hear a parable, you usually hear an argument in process, because the parable is a useful tool for confrontation. Luke, more than Mark or Matthew, has the habit of integrating each parable into his narrative discourse by providing a context of conflict aimed at helping his readers interpret the meaning of the parable. For example:

❖ *Conflict*: "Why do you call me 'Lord, Lord,' and do not do what I tell you?" (Lk 6:46)
   Parable: The Two Builders

❖ *Conflict*: How Simon the Pharisee sees the woman who anoints Jesus (Lk 7:39)
   Parable: The Two Debtors

❖ *Conflict:* "But wanting to justify himself, he asked Jesus, 'And who is my neighbour?'" (Lk 10:29)
   Parable: The Good Samaritan

❖ *Conflict:* The Pharisees and scribes complain that Jesus welcomes and eats with sinners (Lk 15:2)
   Parables: The Lost Sheep; the Lost Coin; the Prodigal Son

❖ *Conflict*: Some people pride themselves on being virtuous while holding others in contempt (Lk 18:9)
   Parable: The Pharisee and the Toll Collector

It may be useful to see how the setting described by Luke for Jesus' controversy with the Pharisees and scribes (Lk 15:2) is mirrored in the third parable, usually entitled The Prodigal Son. Two groups approach Jesus with different purposes. The first group, the tax collectors and sinners, come near to listen to Jesus. The second group, the Pharisees and scribes, come to register their complaint that Jesus welcomes sinners and eats with them. The conflict between Jesus and the Pharisees is focused on their different pastoral strategy towards sinners: Jesus associates with sinners and eats with them, in the hope that his act of hospitality will provide a setting for their repentance; the Pharisees stay separate from sinners, refusing to associate or eat with them until they have repented.

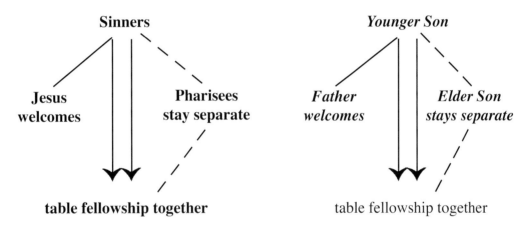

The way Luke develops the argument is by showing how Jesus focuses on a relationship that will support the pastoral challenge to change. It is very difficult to help people to change if you refuse to have any contact with them. The Pharisees do not associate with sinners; they wait until sinners correct their ways – then they will eat with them. This profound pastoral difference between Jesus and the Pharisees is mirrored in the parable where two different ways of responding to failure and sin are explored. The father takes the initiative and runs to be gracious, welcoming his lost son to table fellowship; the elder son, by contrast, stays outside the house, justifying his hostility in argument. All three characters belong to the same world, the same race, the same tribe, and the same family. But only one of them exemplifies the radical values of Jesus within their shared world.

In the parable what is contrasted is not this world versus another world: the contrast is not between worlds but between different ways of being in the same world. That contrast, according to Luke, is at the heart of Jesus' conflict with the Pharisees. There is no suggestion by Luke that the parable resolves the conflict that provokes the telling – the conflict is not resolved within the parable itself, which is deliberately open-ended. Rather, the parable as it stands in Luke's narrative serves to highlight the real conflict indirectly, through the medium of fiction, leaving the challenge to table fellowship open in the parable as it remains open in everyday life.

The parable as subversive teaching

The meaning of any parable is not transparent since the parable, by definition, uses coded language to make its point. Coded language may be used by someone not only as a way of confronting others indirectly but as a necessary safeguard against those in power who will not brook criticism or opposition. In some societies, churches and organisations criticism that is forthright and open is simply not tolerated; if criticism is made, it has to be made indirectly if the critic is to survive another day. For example, in his early work Alexander Solzhenitsyn used fiction – stories and prose poems – not only to criticise but to mock the academic and spiritual oppression that he saw within the Soviet Union;[7] but with the publication of *The Gulag Archipelago* he was expelled from Russia in 1974. It was a story too far, needing little decoding.

Some parables in the Gospels are clearly coded descriptions of the oppression Jesus sees around him. Take, for example, the account in Mark's Gospel where Jesus makes his protest in the Temple precincts and is then questioned about his activity by the chief priests (Mk 11:15–12:12). Jesus organises a one-man riot in the Temple and expels the money-changers, the merchants, and the pilgrims who are making their lawful purchases. He then overturns the money tables and the seats, a clearly subversive act. Not only that, but Mark writes, "and he would not allow anyone to carry anything through the Temple" (11:16). This verse indicates that, for Mark, Jesus wants to foreclose the whole sacrificial system of the Temple. He is not cleansing the Temple for further use; he is signalling an end to it, so that what is needed for the sacrificial system is dismissed.

Not surprisingly, Mark notes that the Temple authorities "kept looking for a way to kill him" (Mk 11:18). When Jesus returns to the Temple, the authorities approach him, to register their complaint and demand to know: "By what authority are you doing these things?"

Jesus refuses to tell them, but he does tell them the parable of The Wicked Tenants. In the parable the tenants kill the servants and the son who is sent. After the parable Mark says: "When they realised that he had told this parable against them, they wanted to arrest him, but they feared the crowd" (12:12). In Mark's understanding the chief priests can readily decode the subversive purpose of the parable; in response they want not to applaud the parable but to arrest the speaker. It is a parable too far, needing little decoding.

In Mark's stark description of Jesus' ministry in Jerusalem, that parable is a subversive story following a subversive act. Telling parables can be a dangerous, life-threatening business as the story of Jesus testifies. Jesus did not die in his bed from old age but was executed by the Roman authorities with the connivance of the Temple hierarchy. After a brief public ministry Jesus ends up on the cross between two bandits – not because he entertained people with harmless spiritual stories about kingdom come, but because he told dangerous stories which radically challenged what was happening in the real kingdoms of his own time. The religious and civil authorities would hardly have judged Jesus as a subversive and a serious threat to order if all he was doing was teaching people about the inner life. The crucifixion of Jesus is a permanent reminder that whatever theory is advanced to explain Jesus' parables, it has to account for the inescapable fact that the one who spoke in parables was publicly executed, under the title "King of the Jews", *by the highest civil authority.*

The parables and the kingdom

While there is general agreement among scholars that the kingdom of God was central to the preaching and teaching of the historical Jesus, there is an equally ready acknowledgement that it is difficult to be precise about the origins of the phrase and its precise meaning. In the Hebrew canon of the Old Testament the phrase "kingdom of God" (which literally translates the Greek *hē basileia tou theou*) never occurs, although there are references to "kingship" and "kingdom". These passages show that God was imagined as the reigning king over Israel, all peoples, and the whole of creation. Although the exact phrase "kingdom of God" is absent, the idea of the supremacy of God's kingly rule and power is well attested. The references are mainly from the later books of the Hebrew canon, which has led J.P. Meier to observe: "To judge from the sparse and late Old Testament evidence, Jesus apparently took up a relatively recent way of referring to God's kingly rule, and he may well have been the first to forge and employ regularly the fixed phrase 'kingdom of God' to evoke the Old Testament mythic story."[8]

For most people the term "kingdom" suggests a territory or region, where subjects are ruled over by a king or other leader. The primary emphasis of the original Semitic word was not a *territory* but the *dynamic activity of God* in which his kingly rule was revealed. The kingdom as God's power and mighty deeds is clearly celebrated in Psalm 145:11-12:

> They shall speak of the glory of your kingdom,
> and tell of your power,
> to make known to all people your mighty deeds
> and the glorious splendour of your kingdom.

This understanding of kingdom as dynamic activity is emphasised by N. Perrin when he writes: "The Kingdom of God is the power of God expressed in deeds; it is that which God does wherein it becomes evident that he is king. It is not a place or community ruled by God; it is not even the abstract idea of reign or kingship of God. It is quite concretely the activity of God as king." [9] While one can accept Perrin's point as a way of emphasising the primary tradition of the kingdom as God's activity, some sayings of Jesus also speak of kingdom in territorial terms such as, "Children, how hard it is to enter the kingdom of God" (Mk 10:24).

In a later work, which has influenced scholarly thinking on the subject of the kingdom, N. Perrin stressed the ambiguity of the phrase "kingdom of God" by speaking of it as a "tensive symbol".[10] A steno symbol has a single relation to what it describes; a tensive symbol evokes a whole range of meanings and cannot be limited to a one-to-one relation to what it describes. To speak of the kingdom of God as a tensive symbol is to acknowledge that one clear image or definition cannot capture the kingdom; the reality of the kingdom is explored through many stories rather than understood through one definition. The tensive symbol that is "the kingdom of God" is not exhausted by one meaning; it defies limitation by preserving its essential ambivalence and open-endedness. This does not empty the symbol of meaning, but serves as a warning against a single, authoritative interpretation.

That ambivalence is evident when we try to answer the question: is the kingdom a future event or a present reality? There is evidence of the historical Jesus seeing the kingdom as future. For example:

❖ When Jesus teaches his disciples to pray "Your kingdom come" – petitioning God to come in the future and rule as king.

❖ When Jesus teaches in the beatitudes that those who suffer and are oppressed will enjoy a reversal of fortune and receive a reward in the kingdom of heaven (Mt 5:3-12; Lk 6:20-23).

❖ When Jesus prophesies that people will come from east and west and recline at table with the patriarchs in the kingdom of God (Mt 8:11-12; Lk 13:28-29).

❖ When Jesus tells his disciples at the last supper that he will not drink the fruit of the vine until the kingdom of God comes (Mk 14:25; Lk 22:18).

There is also evidence in the Gospels that Jesus spoke of the kingdom of God as already present through his words and deeds. For example:

◆ When the imprisoned John the Baptist sends his disciples to ask Jesus if he is the coming one or not, Jesus replies by pointing to his own deeds and words as the fulfilment of Isaiah's prophecies. Although John is great, the least in the kingdom – those experiencing the power of Jesus' ministry – are greater than John (Mt 11:2-19; Lk 7:18-23).

◆ When Jesus speaks of John the Baptist as the transition figure between the time of the law and the prophets and the new time of the kingdom of God, which is now subject to violent opposition in Jesus' ministry (Mt 11:7-11; Lk 7:24-28).

◆ When Jesus refers to his exorcisms by saying that if it is by the finger of God that he casts out demons then the kingdom of God has already come upon people (Mt 12:28; Lk 11:20).

◆ When Jesus is asked by the Pharisees when the kingdom is coming, he replies that the kingdom of God is already in their midst (Lk 17:20-21).

Jesus' teaching about the kingdom as present yet future, already but not yet, remains stubbornly paradoxical and does not yield to a ready understanding. While this admission is not an explanation, it preserves Jesus' double usage without eliminating one in the hope of clarifying the other.

Jesus spoke of the kingdom as already *present* in some form through the agency of his own person – not only in his teaching, which had immediate consequences in the lives of his listeners, but in his liberating actions, particularly his table fellowship with toll collectors and sinners, and in his ministry of healing and exorcism. Yet his preferred way of speaking about the *future* was through the symbol of the kingdom of God – not the future as wholly other from the present, but the future as the context in which the present could be both criticised and renewed. It is little wonder then that the chosen vehicle of Jesus' teaching on the kingdom was the parable, itself an oblique form of communication.

Throughout the pages of the Gospel, when Jesus speaks about the kingdom he never defines what the kingdom actually is but offers extended metaphors and similes that attempt to catch something of what the kingdom is like: "The kingdom is like a . . ." Speaking about the kingdom, Jesus throws a story beside his subject: a multifaceted symbol is now given a particular focus through parable. The word parable comes from the Greek, *parabolē* (literally: beside/throw), meaning to throw something beside something else, to compare, to show how different things are like one another. The writer of the song "You are my sunshine" takes the dissimilar ("you" and "sunshine") and throws them side by side in a metaphor. This strange interaction, however resistant to rational analysis, seeks to spark off a new understanding and to celebrate the joy someone experiences in the presence of the other, a joy that goes beyond the limits of ordinary language.

We all have to face the limits of language when we try to express what we think and feel, especially when we try to find language that will go some way to express our love and our deepest beliefs. As T.S. Eliot noted with parabolic brevity:

> It's strange that words are so inadequate.
> Yet, like an asthmatic struggling for breath,
> So the lover must struggle for words.

Every parable struggles to express a particular truth or insight through imagery. The teaching of Jesus on the kingdom of God, while not limited to parables, has its most popular expression in that form of indirect communication. The purpose of speaking in parables is not to envelop difficult teaching in impenetrable storytelling – bewildering people is not a pastoral art – but to reveal an important truth by stealth. As S. TeSelle observes: "The point is that difficult, strange, unfamiliar matters must be approached with the utmost cunning, imagination and indirection for them to be seen at all . . . We are always children, primitives, when it comes to insight into such matters as love, life, death, God, hope, and faith. The point is, of course, that apart from metaphor, that is, apart from primal language, we would not 'see' such matters at all but would be like the rest of creation – dumb and univocal, knowing but one reference for each sign."[11]

While TeSelle's point is well made – the metaphor is a primal way of moving to new meaning – it is not only unfamiliar matters that must be approached with "cunning, imagination and indirection". All too familiar matters, especially structures of oppression that are protected by authority, need to be approached with artfulness and coded language if the critics are to survive the dissension they express. The parable provides a veil for dangerous revelation about familiar matters. Jesus' teaching on the kingdom of God will inevitably stir up opposition, which is one reason the parable form will prove a useful tool. One of the functions of the parable will be to confront the neglect and oppression Jesus sees in the kingdoms around him with the values of the kingdom of God. Thus the parable is the privileged way Jesus uses to speak of the kingdom of God.

The language of the parable

The parables of Jesus emerge from an oral culture, where it is not only faith that comes by hearing but almost every form of education and enlightenment. The great loss in oral culture is forgetting what you have heard, so, as Walter Ong points out in his study of orality and literacy, it is important to communicate memorable thoughts that can be recalled easily.[12] Vivid, pictorial language, rather than abstract thought, becomes the normal vehicle of communication because that kind of language is easy to remember and the best way of fighting forgetfulness.

a) Pictorial speech

This way of speaking helps the hearer to see, to imagine, and to feel. If someone asks you how you are, you could say, "My metabolism is not responding to the stimulation of food." That may be an accurate recital of your condition but it lacks any description of how you actually feel. The oral tradition uses vivid language to speak concretely to its hearers; it aims for immediate engagement rather than leisurely philosophical reflection. Given that the parables are short narrative fiction, their performance is intense and brief. They are not followed by lengthy commentary, any more than poets attach commentaries to their poems:

as the meaning of the poem is in the poem, so the meaning of the parable is in the parable. The parables' brevity and pictorial language are aimed at fixing their chosen issues in our memory and imagination.

b) The role of conflict and contrast
When the American film director John Ford was interviewed about his technique for making westerns, he stated that there was only one way to open a film to arouse people's interest. You must begin, he said, by having a stranger ride at full gallop into town. The peaceful life of the settlement is going to be disturbed by this stranger. The townspeople don't know who he is; they don't know where he is coming from; they have no idea why he is in such a hurry. And why *here*? For Ford, all these questions were provoked by the arrival of a stranger who kicked up so much dust. The life of the settlement was primed for conflict; there was the making of a story.

All stories progress by way of conflict; while some conclude with resolution, others are deliberately left open-ended. "Once upon a time everyone lived happily ever after" is not a story, but the absence of story. If you watch a film or read a novel, the opening format is predictably the same as ancient storytelling: something goes wrong quickly. This establishes the plot and immediately introduces a series of questions. How are people going to react in this situation? How are they going to relate to one another? How is the problem going to be solved? Hence the immediate conflict in the parables: a shepherd loses a sheep; a housewife loses a coin; people invited to a banquet refuse to turn up; a widow is refused justice; a friend arrives unannounced, etc. These problems arouse our interest in the brief ensuing drama.

Storytelling also needs contrast and variety; it needs difference if the story is to proceed. So in the parables you find the contrast between virtue and vice, wisdom and stupidity, graciousness and meanness, poverty and plenty. In the stories of Jesus we are invited to enter a visual world of dinner parties, sheepfolds, vineyards, welcome households, dangerous journeys. It is a world of great variety. You meet all sorts of people: difficult judges, committed burglars, broken families, wounded beggars, awkward neighbours, selfish priests, eccentric employers, desperate hosts, surprised guests, wise and foolish virgins.

You see how differently people act and react: with generosity, with fear, with delight, with suspicion, with jealousy, with energy, with open arms, with closed hearts. We are invited not only to think but also to feel, to find ourselves somewhere inside the story, to be questioned by the issues it raises.

c) *Language as event*

While the parables found in the Gospels can be scrutinised and explored by literary criticism, in their original setting they were "language events"[13] aimed at changing the hearer's mind. A.M. Hunter emphasised the point when he wrote:

> A successful parable is an event in two ways: (1) It creates a new possibility in the situation; and (2) it compels the hearer to decide in one way or the other. In his parable the teller risks everything on the power of language. Moreover, the deeper opposition between the teller and his hearer, the bigger the decision facing the hearer. And there are oppositions which go right down beneath a man's conscious state of mind to the depth of his very being and involve all his acts and attitudes. To such situations – and oppositions – Jesus parables were commonly directed.[14]

If the parables work, they leave us wondering not just about the dynamics of an interesting story but about deeply personal and social questions we face every day. Parables are not fictional diversions from real life but deliberate probes into the lives we actually live. They call us to think again about how we see and how we behave, to think again about attitudes and behaviour in our community or society that we accept lazily or uncritically. The parables of Jesus *make the ordinary important:* Jesus speaks out of a theology of ordinariness when he begins his theological thinking with things as they are. Religion is not primarily about special cultic activities or secret wisdom; it is about loving the God who created us and loving the neighbour we find ourselves beside. Liturgy can be left to one side when more important business, like forgiving our brother or sister, is waiting as the real religious agenda.

In Jesus' parables there is a marked absence of the supernatural. Jesus baptises the ordinary and tells us that it is in the theatre of the ordinary that the drama of salvation is being lived out. By calling on everyday experience, the parables tell us that we are saved where we are. Salvation is primarily something that happens to people in the midst of life. The word that Jesus often puts beside salvation is

"Today". Thus he meets the cautious repentance of Zacchaeus with the generous word of Gospel: "Today salvation has come to this house" (Lk 19:9).

In the parables we are invited to make a choice and come to a decision; we are commanded to pay attention and face issues we might prefer to ignore. The parables tell us that it is in the midst of the everyday – the regular, mundane business of our eating, drinking, sleeping, choosing, loving, forgiving, reaching out, journeying, noticing people, answering doors, offering hospitality, sharing bread, and listening to midnight stories – that our happiness and salvation are being worked out. Through the parables we learn that inside the story of our everyday life lies the deeper story of our salvation.

[1] M. Goldberg, *Theology and Narrative: a Critical Introduction* (Nashville: Abingdon, 1982) p.36

[2] The table is offered as a summary of types of story based on the discussion in W.R. Herzog, *Parables as Subversive Speech: Jesus as Pedagogue of the Oppressed* (Westminster: John Knox Press, 1994) pp.44-51; J.D. Crossan, *The Dark Interval: Towards a Theology of Story* (Illinois: Argus Communications, 1975) pp.47-62. Both discussions are indebted to the seminal work of S. Sacks, *Fiction and the Shape of Belief* (Berkeley: University of California Press, 1967).

[3] J.D. Crossan, *The Dark Interval: Towards a Theology of Story*, p.60

[4] E. Wiesel, *Legends of our Time* (New York: Avon Books, 1970) p.viii

[5] J. Jeremias, *The Parables of Jesus* (London: SCM, 1972) p.21

[6] W.H. Vanstone, *Fare Well in Christ* (London: DLT, 1997) p.32

[7] See, for example, "Lake Segden" in A. Solzhenitsyn, *Stories and Poems* (London: Bodley Head, 1970) pp.227-229

[8] J.P. Meier, *A Marginal Jew: Rethinking the Historical Jesus* Vol 2 (New York: Doubleday, 1994) p.244

[9] N. Perrin, *Rediscovering the Teaching of Jesus* (London: SCM, 1967) p.55

[10] N. Perrin, *Jesus and the Language of the Kingdom* (Philadelphia: Fortress, 1976) pp.29-34. Perrin borrowed the distinction between steno and tensive symbols from P. Wheelwright's work, *Metaphor and Reality* (Bloomington: Indiana University Press, 1962)

[11] S. TeSelle, *Speaking in Parables: a Study of Metaphor and Theology* (Philadelphia: Fortress, 1975) pp.40-41

[12] W. Ong, *Orality and Literacy* (New York: Methuen, 1982) pp.16-30

[13] See E. Linnemann, *Jesus of the Parables* (New York: Harper & Row, 1966) pp.30-33

[14] A.M. Hunter, *The Parables Then and Now* (London: SCM, 1971) pp.11-12

Matthew 25:31-46 (RSV)

[31]*"When the Son of man comes in his glory, and all the angels with him, then he will sit on his glorious throne.* [32]*Before him will be gathered all the nations, and he will separate them one from another as a shepherd separates the sheep from the goats,* [33]*and he will place the sheep at his right hand, but the goats at the left.* [34]*Then the King will say to those at his right hand, 'Come, O blessed of my Father, inherit the kingdom prepared for you from the foundation of the world;* [35]*for I was hungry and you gave me food, I was thirsty and you gave me drink, I was a stranger and you welcomed me,* [36]*I was naked and you clothed me, I was sick and you visited me, I was in prison and you came to me.'* [37]*Then the righteous will answer him, 'Lord, when did we see thee hungry and feed thee, or thirsty and give thee drink?* [38]*And when did we see thee a stranger and welcome thee, or naked and clothe thee?* [39]*And when did we see thee sick or in prison and visit thee?'* [40]*And the King will answer them, 'Truly, I say to you, as you did it to one of the least of these my brethren, you did it to me.'*

[41]*Then he will say to those at his left hand, 'Depart from me, you cursed, into the eternal fire prepared for the devil and his angels;* [42]*for I was hungry and you gave me no food, I was thirsty and you gave me no drink,* [43]*I was a stranger and you did not welcome me, naked and you did not clothe me, sick and in prison and you did not visit me.'* [44]*Then they also will answer, 'Lord, when did we see thee hungry or thirsty or a stranger or naked or sick or in prison, and did not minister to thee?'* [45]*Then he will answer them, 'Truly, I say to you, as you did it not to one of the least of these, you did it not to me.'* [46]*And they will go away into eternal punishment, but the righteous into eternal life."*

Beginning at the end

It may seem strange to begin our exploration of the parables with a text that, arguably, cannot properly be called a parable since it is in the form of an apocalyptic vision of the last judgement. As the climax of the fifth and final discourse of Matthew's Gospel, however, The Last Judgement focuses on a number of human values that are honoured as fundamental in securing a welcome into the kingdom. Its inclusion at the beginning of this book is deliberate because of its universalism and since it hallows a core of human values, using good works as the criterion of judgement, which will be found in a number of parables.

Matthew's arrangement of Jesus' final discourse moves between the local and the universal: beginning with the destruction of the Temple in Jerusalem, it moves through a catalogue of natural and international disasters that will lead up to the parousia and the coming of the Son of Man. The discourse then goes on, through a series of parables, to warn the disciples to be constantly alert and prepared, climaxing in the final judgement of all nations, where true vigilance is revealed, to the surprise of everyone, to be a life of love and mercy. Matthew's structure can be seen in the following division:

> *Introduction*: The Destruction of the Temple (24:1-2)
>> The Beginning of the End (24:3-8)
>> The Effects of Persecution (24:9-14)
>> Tribulation in Judea; False Prophets (24:15-28)
>> The Coming of the Son of Man (24:29-31)
>> The Parable of the Fig Tree (24:32-36)
>> The Parable of the Flood (24:37-42)
>> The Parable of the Thief in the Night (24:43-44)
>> The Parable of the Prudent and the Villainous Slaves (24:45-51)
>> The Parable of the Ten Virgins (25:1-13)
>> The Parable of the Talents (25:14-30)
> *Conclusion*: The Last Judgement (25:31-46)

The discourse is given only to the disciples and has its climax in the apocalyptic vision of the last judgement. Apocalypse may seem a strange place for us to begin, but endings can make for new beginnings: *the future is revealed to help us to live genuine lives today*. The Greek word *apokalypsis* literally means uncovering; it is the act of removing the covering that conceals something, thereby exposing it to view. The apocalyptic vision of The Last Judgement unveils a truth that is hidden – not to satisfy any fitful curiosity about the future tense but to challenge us, hearers and readers, about the values we live by in the present tense. The Last Judgement provokes the question: if that is how we will be judged at the end of time, how should we live our lives today?

The Last Judgement refuses to see the future as an accident of fate or humanity as its hapless victims; rather, it uncovers the truth that our future will be the direct consequence of the everyday choices we make. In that sense the teaching attempts to make us *conscious* choice-makers in favour of the disadvantaged. Who we become in the fullness of time will depend on the choices we make and the values we choose to govern out lives.

Background: power and discipleship

The challenge to favour the disadvantaged is not a new theme in Matthew's Gospel. Matthew devotes the whole of chapter 18, the famous sermon on church order and life, to the questions of authority and pastoral responsibility. The chapter opens with the disciples' question: "Who is the greatest in the kingdom of heaven?" While Matthew alters Mark's setting of conflict – where the disciples follow Jesus out of earshot while they argue among themselves which of them is the greatest (Mk 9:33-37) – Matthew retains the disciples' preoccupation with hierarchy to set the scene for Jesus' contrary teaching on authority.

The question posed by the disciples is clearly not an academic one, for it prompts Jesus to call the questioners to conversion, charging them to turn from their fascination with primacy, hierarchy and power to making themselves little, like a child. The ensuing warning is unambiguous: unless they do this, they cannot enter the kingdom (Mt 18:3). Where Mark has Jesus enjoin the disciples to *welcome* the little ones, Matthew has Jesus charge them to *become* like them, namely, model themselves on those who are simple and unpretentious, those without power and prestige in an adult world.

The sermon goes on to warn the disciples: "See that you do not despise one of these little ones" (Mt 18:10). The little ones are clearly *not* the disciples but those whose plight the disciples might be tempted to ignore. A danger for authority in any organised community is that it attends to the privileged minority and ends up, consciously or unconsciously, holding the legion of the needy in disdain because they fail to register as important in the barometer of power. Jesus' values reverse that conventional practice: it is the last and the least and the lost who should command the focus of attention from those who exercise power in the name of Jesus, even if that means leaving the ninety-nine who do not stray in order to search for the one who has wandered off or been misled.

By the time Matthew writes his Gospel, probably in Antioch in the mid eighties, he has already had a mixed experience of church authority. As R.E. Brown comments: "Matthew has lived long enough with that authority to know its dangers. Experience teaches that organised societies are more likely to abuse authority than to abdicate it . . . A church that lives and acts according to the spirit of Matt 18 will be a society that is distinct from others, one where what counts for wisdom in other societies has not been able to stifle the voice of Jesus who came to challenge much of the religious wisdom of his time."[1]

Jesus' challenging teaching against lusting after primacy is continued when two of the disciples, James and John, either directly (Mark) or through the agency of their mother (Matthew), seek to stake their claim to pre-eminence by asking to sit at Jesus' right and left in the kingdom (Mt 20:20-28). Being part of the inner circle of three is not enough to satisfy the ambitious brothers; they seek to displace Peter in a bloodless coup. Unsurprisingly, their raw ambition makes the other ten disciples indignant.

In response to the disarray among his disciples, Jesus rejects any comparison between the kind of authority he is asking them to exercise and the way authority is exercised among the Gentiles. Again Jesus clarifies his own subversive thinking on power and discipleship by defining his position over and against models of authority in the surrounding society, thus calling his disciples to be non-conformists. Dominating others, lording it over people, ensuring that others feel your authority, these are dismissed as foreign influences that are wholly inappropriate in Christian leaders. All desire for precedence and privilege is to be excluded; the only greatness the disciple of Jesus should aspire to is that of service to others.

In confronting his disciples in their attitudes to authority and pastoral leadership, Jesus opposes the conventional models that influence his followers, warning them that unless they change they cannot enter the kingdom of heaven (Mt 18:3). Entering the kingdom is not an automatic process for disciples who minister, even work many miracles, in the name of Jesus (Mt 7:21-23). As The Last Judgement will show, entrance to the kingdom for everyone, not just Jesus' audience of disciples, will depend on loving attention to the vulnerable and the needy.

The gathering

The apocalyptic vision of The Last Judgement opens with the enthronement of the Son of Man. Matthew has developed the theme of the coming of the Son of Man throughout Jesus' final discourse to his disciples on the mount of Olives, and establishes from the beginning that this is the coming of *Jesus*: "what will be the sign of your coming and of the close of the age?" (Mt 24:3). Prior to the teaching of The Last Judgement, Matthew has described the coming of the Son of Man as follows:

> *it will be sudden and clear as lightning (24:27)*
> *the Son of Man will come with power and great glory (24:30)*
> *the angels will gather his elect from the four winds (24:31)*
> *only the Father knows the day and the hour (24:36)*
> *the coming will be a surprise, like a thief in the night (24:43)*
> *it will be a time of reckoning and punishment (24:45-51)*
> *it may be delayed, so everyone must be watchful (25:1-13)*

The Last Judgement envisions the actual coming of the Son of Man in divine majesty, when he appears in *his* glory, with the angels having no other part than as *his* heavenly escort as he takes his seat on *his* throne of glory. This solemn enthronement scene reveals the Son of Man as the one who presides over all the nations (*panta ta ethnē*) – not just the Gentile people. Some scholars argue that it is only the Gentiles who are being judged, while others argue that it is Christians. S. Gray lists thirty-two variously nuanced positions in his survey of the history of interpretation of The Last Judgement, a caution that the meaning of this passage has always provoked vigorous debate.[2]

While it is true that elsewhere in his Gospel Matthew does not use the phrase "the nations" to refer to Christians or even to Christians and non-Christians together, it can be argued that the shift in his narrative to an apocalyptic vision of final judgement transposes the meaning to a universalist key. It could be said that the dominant theme of Matthew's writing is the movement from the *particularist* preaching of Jesus ("I was sent only to the lost sheep of the house of Israel" 15:24) to the *universalist* preaching of the infant church ("Go therefore and make disciples of all nations" 28:19). The final command of the risen Jesus does not exclude continuing to preach the Gospel to the Jews; rather, it extends the reach of that preaching to make it truly catholic. Just as the course of Matthew's narrative acts as a vigorous defence for moving the preaching of the Gospel ever outwards to embrace everyone, without exception, I think the final discourse follows the same movement, concluding with a final judgement that embraces everyone, without exception.

The gathering is the assembly of humanity, presided over by the supreme king of all peoples who has taken his seat on his glorious throne. He has dominion over all and has, therefore, the right to judge all, a right that has been conferred on him by God: "All authority in heaven and on earth has been given to me" (Mt 28:18). Among those who are assembled there is no distinction or discrimination between races or religions, between Jew and Gentile, between priest and lay, between man and woman. There is no hierarchy, no privilege, and no precedence. What the assembled people share is their common bond of humanity, so that when the king/shepherd makes the separation, he will be separating the people as individuals not as national or religious groupings.

The separation and the judgement

Although this is a judgement scene, there is no trial procedure. The trial has taken place during the life of each person and the judgement has already been made; the only outstanding business is to pass sentence. The imagery shifts momentarily from king to shepherd to match the parabolic imagery of the assembly as a gathered flock. The image of a shepherd separating sheep from goats was a regular, rather than a final occurrence in Palestinian life. As J. Jeremias notes: "The Palestinian shepherd does not separate sheep from rams (i.e. the females from the males), but sheep from the goats, since the goats need to be kept warm at night, for cold harms them, while the sheep prefer open air at night."[3] In the scenario of the parable, however, the separation is final as it constitutes eternal judgement.

The sheep are placed on the right, the goats on the left. The customary use of "right and left understanding" in popular lore is brought into play, where right is distinguished from left as honesty from treachery, blessing from curse, and good fortune from bad luck. Unfortunately for left-handed people, this dualism has been carried into the English language: thus when people's actions are described as dextrous (from the Latin *dexter*, on the right hand) it means that what is done is adroit, skilful, subtle; whereas if what is done is described as sinister (from the Latin *sinister*, on the left hand), it is underhand, malign, suggesting the threat of evil.

The king welcomes those on his right hand with the words: "Come, O blessed of my Father, inherit the kingdom prepared for you from the foundation of the world." Just as the land of Israel was granted by God to his chosen people, so now the new people of God are granted the kingdom as their inheritance. Those who are reckoned blessed take possession of the only kingdom that has outlasted the creation of the world. Throughout the turmoil of history and in spite of the defiance of humankind, God's abiding purpose was never frustrated: his kingdom stands secure and ready for those who have distinguished themselves by acts of mercy.

In the judgement the only division made is between those who connected themselves to the needy and those who remained disconnected from them. People are welcomed as "blessed of my Father" because they have paid attention not to the Father or the Son but to the legion of the vulnerable within their reach. Six categories of people in distress are listed, together with six appropriate responses.

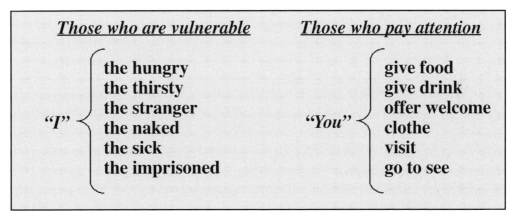

**Those who are vulnerable**		_**Those who pay attention**_	
_"I"_	the hungry	_"You"_	give food
	the thirsty		give drink
	the stranger		offer welcome
	the naked		clothe
	the sick		visit
	the imprisoned		go to see

In the left-hand column there is a list of vulnerable human beings whose needs await recognition and practical help, together with the startling revelation that Jesus' presence abides among them. In the right-hand column there is a list of humane responses by the just, together with the startling revelation that Jesus himself was the beneficiary of these acts of kindness. The blessed are commended for their actions, not their attitudes; for what they did, not for what they thought. Misery obliged them to act, so their active verbs prove to be what is important. Their response was humane and, therefore, profoundly religious; it is hallowed as the kingdom response of those who take responsibility for a broken world.

In his reflections on humanity, the distinguished Jewish philosopher Abraham Heschel makes a distinction between _human being_ and _being human_: while we are all human beings, being human is something we become or fail to become. Humanity is not a given but a goal for every human being. He writes: "The degree to which one is sensitive to other people's suffering, to other men's humanity, is the index of one's own humanity. It is the root not only for social living but for the study of humanities . . . The central problem of biblical thinking is not: 'What is *to be?*' but rather: 'How to be and how not to be?'"[4] That, it seems to me, is the question of The Last Judgement.

The blessed are commended for their humane solidarity with those who suffer loss. No special training or charismatic gift or even religious insight was needed to equip them for their ministry of mercy. They are acclaimed, for example, for doing the ordinary round of visiting the sick and imprisoned, not for the extraordinary ministry of *healing* the afflicted and *liberating* prisoners. The expectation is that these works of mercy are within the capacity of every human being, that all people, no matter what their racial or religious background, can administer this practical care. The blessed did precisely that.

That is why, in this universal judgement, there is no mention of great heroics, no stories of conquest, no tales of remarkable virtue, no outstanding triumphs over disaster; in fact there is no specifically religious note sounded. The actions are the simple response of those who pay attention to what happens in the world of the familiar and who move to answer the needs that confront them. For Jesus, what happens in the world of the familiar has an eternity of importance about it. Human graciousness and kindness are ground enough for welcome into the fullness of the kingdom. In this understanding religion is not about a privatised relationship with God, independent of those who suffer around us. People's suffering is not considered a distraction from God's purposes; rather, their suffering incarnates the agenda for a kingdom people.

Those on the king's left hand are called cursed and then condemned to "the eternal fire prepared for the devil and his angels". Although the imagery of fire for future punishment has no history in ancient Hebrew thought, Matthew has already spoken of the Gehenna of fire (5:22; 18:9). The word Gehenna originally referred to the valley of the Hinnom, a narrow gorge that curves along the west and south of Jerusalem. The valley was the scene of the idolatrous worship of the gods Molech and Baal, who, it was believed, could only be placated by children being burned in sacrifice on "the high place of Topheth" (Jer 7:31; see 19:4-5). The valley's association with fire arose not only from the sacrificial cult of Molech but from the fires that continually burned there when the valley became a rubbish dump. Isaiah prophesied that the site would be readied for Molech himself (Is 30:33), and he spoke about an unquenchable fire prepared for the wicked (Is 33:14; 66:24). By the first century AD, however, Gehenna had become divorced from its geographical location as a rubbish dump to become hell itself.

As the blessed were not praised for heroic virtues, the cursed are not accused of great offences or violent crimes: they are condemned because of their failure to be humane to those in need. The principle of judgement is the same for everyone, and the list of the needy remains unchanged.

The protest: "When did we see you … ?"

Those who are blessed are not conscious of having done any special service to the king (Jesus). Their surprise is expressed by the question "But when did we see you … ?" Commenting on Egyptian and rabbinic parallels, J. Jeremias observes: "Both in the Egyptian Book of the Dead and in the Midrash the dead man boasts self-confidently of his good deeds ('I have given satisfaction to God by doing that in which he delights: I have given bread to the hungry, water to the thirsty, clothed the naked …') How differently sounds the surprised question of the righteous, who are unconscious of having rendered any service, to say nothing of the conception that in the persons of the poor and wretched, men are confronted by the hidden Messiah."[5] The surprise is, of course, shared by the condemned who voice the same question.

The blessed are astounded at the revelation that the king identifies himself with the needy, and they protest that they never saw *him* when they performed their works of mercy. They were never conscious of ministering to Jesus, only to the needy. The king explains in his answer: "Truly, I say to you, as you did it to one of the least of these my brethren, you did it to me." Who are the king's brethren? Are they the same people as the needy? Or are they disciples/missionaries who form a persecuted minority within society at large?

Those who hold the latter position usually argue that the final judgement is a judgement of *Gentiles* who are held accountable for the way they have treated *disciples of Jesus*. This interpretation reduces the sweeping universalism of The Last Judgement to a letter of consolation to Christians who are facing neglect or threat from the surrounding Gentile society. In this rendering the blessed are identified as those Gentiles who attended to Jesus' disciples when they were in need; their merciful attention to the least of Jesus' brethren proves to be acceptance of Jesus himself. Certainly, in the course of Matthew's Gospel, it is clear that Jesus identifies himself with his disciples: "He who receives you receives me, and he who receives me receives him who sent me … And whoever gives to one of these little ones even a cup of cold water because he is a disciple, truly, I say to you, he shall not lose his reward" (Mt 10:40, 42). Jesus' identification with his disciples in Matthew's writing leads G. Stanton to conclude: "In short, whereas early Christian writings do not identify Jesus with the poor and needy, the close identification of Jesus with his disciples is a thoroughly Matthean theme which is also found elsewhere."[6]

Jesus' identification with his disciples and their identification with him do not make for *surprise*, particularly when the early Christian proclamation focused on the death and resurrection of Jesus. In stark contrast, the only response of the assembly is their concerted *surprise*, expressed as protest, that Jesus identifies himself with the needy. That surprise is part of the teaching of The Last Judgement. I find it difficult to accept the identification of the needy as disciples because that reading seems inconsistent with the whole gathering's surprise and ignorance, so essential to the dynamic of the story. Surely the just would have known that when they welcomed Christian missionaries they were also welcoming the one who sent them? Both the blessed and the condemned profess their ignorance of the connection between the people they served or failed to serve and the person of Jesus. If "the least of my brethren" were indeed Christian missionaries welcomed for preaching the Gospel, it seems hard to believe that the Gentiles would have remained so steadfastly ignorant of the very person the missionaries were proclaiming. This is all the more puzzling precisely because of Jesus' identification with his disciples and their identification with him.

The surprise and the ignorance of the whole gathering are more consistent with a judgement of all peoples who are being held accountable for their relationship with the needy of the world. The assembly's surprise, it may be said, may also be reflected in the reader's astonishment that Jesus has chosen to identify himself so closely with the needy among humanity. We as Christians are not beyond astonishment in regard to that particular revelation!

As we noted at the beginning of this chapter, Jesus allied himself with the little child over against the disciples in their concern for primacy (Mt 18:1-6); he asked his followers not to despise the little ones (18:10); he challenged them to change their way of thinking about pastoral leadership and become servants: "Whoever would be great among you must be your servant" (Mt 20:26). As J.P. Meier comments: "Here (in the Last Judgement scene) it becomes clear that 'servant' cannot evaporate into another hierarchical title; service means the concrete performance of the loving acts listed (cf. 16:27). Because the second group has neglected such acts, it neglected the Son of Man; and so its neglect has become fatal . . . Christ's teaching on the twofold love of God and neighbour (22:34-40) thus undergoes a profound transformation: love of the (poor) neighbour is practically identified with love of God and receives a christological basis."[7] That christological basis, it seems to me, is the heart of the parable's subversive teaching: kindness to the needy proves to be real attentiveness to Jesus.

Reflection

At the centre of The Last Judgement is the revelation that one way Jesus elects to be present to humanity is through the cry of the needy. His "I" is hidden in what might be regarded as a most unlikely sanctuary. Imagine for a moment three alien travellers journeying from outer space aboard their starship: they are coming with the express intention of finding an unusual king who is rumoured to be living among us. The three pilgrims land unannounced on our doorstep, carrying the gifts they have brought from afar, and tell us why they have journeyed to this place: they are looking for Jesus. We cannot help but notice their curious gifts and wonder what possible use anyone could find for them, but we say nothing. Their question brings us back to their purpose: "Where," they ask, "can we find him?"

What directions would we give? We might direct them to the church, in the hope that the priests might introduce them to word and sacrament. Or we might direct them to strange sanctuaries, such as refugee camps and hospitals and prisons, and say that Jesus himself said that he was to be found among the inhabitants there. Granted, this is a bizarre scene, but it is not the visit of the aliens that makes it so.

In the apocalyptic vision of The Last Judgement, given to the disciples prior to his death, Jesus focuses attention on his continuing presence among the needy. It is as if Jesus deliberately turns his own followers away from an exclusive attraction to himself, away from a restricted focus on his own person, to look elsewhere to find him. In so doing, he challenges us to face the pain and loss endured by others, not keep staring at him. He will be found where others suffer.

In the parable Jesus reveals his own profound respect for those who suffer in the midst of life. At the same time he hallows the many ordinary kindnesses of those who have never heard of him – the vast majority of humankind – and claims that the way of mercy is a way to the fullness of the kingdom. The parable answers the question Christians sometimes ask: What will happen to all those unbaptised who have never heard of Jesus the Christ, those who have never "seen" him? The parable answers that they have all met him because he has been hiding unseen in the vulnerable people they encountered in the course of their lives. There are many roads to God: mercy to the legion of the needy is one of the most sure.

When we allow the parable to interpret us, we recognise that sometimes we are in the right-hand column – among those who try to pay attention and stay connected to the vulnerable. There are times, of course, when we ignore them; but there are times when we inhabit the left-hand column, when we live among those who hunger and thirst – not for food and drink, perhaps, but for other basic essentials that give life.

We hunger and thirst	*to be wanted and to be loved*
	to be affirmed and encouraged
	to live in peace and know justice
We are naked	*when everyone knows our failure*
	when we are exposed in our sin/weakness
	when we lose our good name
We are the stranger	*when we feel like the permanent outsider*
	when we are excluded because of
	our colour/our race/our religion/our difference
	when we are ignored
We are sick	*when we are burdened by anxiety or loss*
	when sadness is upon us
	when we are broken-hearted or depressed
We are imprisoned	*when we are shut inside our own loneliness*
	when we feel hemmed in by life and misfortune
	when we live in permanent unemployment

When we live inside our own suffering and loss we hope that others will pay attention, that they will notice our plight and minister to us, that they will share their resources and resourcefulness with us. And when they do, we always welcome their attention and kindness as good news. When we suffer *we* know what good news would be for us: *our suffering defines the meaning of Gospel.*

Before her death, Mother Teresa of Calcutta told a BBC interviewer why she spent her long life in caring for the rejects of society: "I have said this many times before but I will say it again: Jesus is present in the broken bodies of these suffering people. My way of serving him is to serve them. The biggest disease in the world today is not leprosy or AIDS, but the feeling of being unwanted and uncared for. The greatest evil is the lack of love, the terrible indifference towards one's neighbour. What the poor, and not just the poor, need even more than food, clothes and shelter, is to be wanted." Her stubborn work on behalf of the needy, and the work of those like her, might provide the most eloquent commentary on the teaching of The Last Judgement.

---

[1] R.E. Brown, *The Churches the Apostles Left Behind* (London: Chapman, 1984) p.145

[2] S.W. Gray, *The Least of My Brothers: Matthew 25:31-46: A History of Interpretation* (Atlanta: SBLDS, 1989)

[3] J. Jeremias, *The Parables of Jesus*, p.206

[4] A.J. Heschel, *Who is Man?* (California: Stanford University Press, 1975) pp.46-47

[5] J. Jeremias, *The Parables of Jesus*, p.208

[6] G.N. Stanton, *A Gospel for a New People: Studies in Matthew* (Edinburgh: T & T Clark, 1993) pp.217-218. See also J.M. Court, "Right and Left: the Implications for Matthew 25:31-46" in *New Testament Studies* 31(1985) pp.223-233

[7] J.P. Meier, *Matthew* (Dublin: Veritas, 1981) p.305

Jesus and table fellowship

All four Gospels agree that Jesus begins his ministry after John the Baptist. The evangelists present both John and Jesus as independent, nomadic prophets whose authority is not mediated by any human organisation or derived, like rabbis and scribes, from studying the scriptures. While both men may be at home in the Jewish scriptures, neither attracts followers or students because of their study or authoritative interpretation. Although John and Jesus do not attach themselves to any particular religious institution or group, both attract and retain their own followers. The chief priests, the elders and the scribes question Jesus about his authority: "By what authority are you doing these things, or who gave you this authority to do them?" (Mk 11:28). Jesus counters with his own question about the origin of John's baptism, refusing to answer the question about the origin of his own authority.

A composite picture emerges from the Gospels of John as a charismatic leader whose great popularity among the people is exercised apart from Jesus. His ministry begins before Jesus, and when John dies he leaves behind him a religious following that exists independently of Christianity. John's ministry dominates the beginning of the Gospel, and Jesus submits to John's baptism of repentance for the forgiveness of sins. As an independent nomadic prophet, John displays no discernible respect for religious hierarchy and he appears alienated from institutional religion. His natural sanctuary is the wilderness, not the Temple; his ritual act centres around the waters of the river, not around the priestly altar of sacrifice. John's alienation from normal society is underscored by his ascetic lifestyle in an uninhabited place, his Bedouin dress of animal skin and his peasant diet of locusts and wild honey. The composite picture of John and his ministry that emerges from the Gospels seems to set a stage of conflict, one that Jesus will enter on the side of John:

the city of Jerusalem	**versus**	**the wilderness**
the Temple (sacrifice)	**versus**	**River Jordan (baptism)**
the priestly (altar)	**versus**	**the prophetic (word of God)**
the institutional	**versus**	**the charismatic**
the temporal power	**versus**	**the religious critic**
the aristocracy	**versus**	**the marginalised**
the settled	**versus**	**the nomadic**

While Jesus begins his ministry following in the footsteps of John the Baptist – so much so that ordinary people and Herod confuse Jesus with John (Mk 6:14-16) – it soon emerges that there is a marked difference between the two men in their message, their methods of pastoral outreach, and their lifestyle. John is a preacher of repentance, challenging people to change their ways, thus avoiding the retribution by fire that is to come; he invites the people to undergo a baptism for the forgiveness of sins; he lives an ascetic lifestyle in the wilderness. Jesus, by contrast, proclaims a Gospel of love and mercy, a message that is confirmed through his ministry of healing and forgiveness; he eats and drinks with toll collectors and sinners in towns and villages.

Jesus' practice of table fellowship with sinners sets him apart not only from John but also from all the contemporary religious groupings within Judaism. It is a unique mark of his ministry, one which causes scandal and draws open criticism: "And they said to him, 'The disciples of John fast often and offer prayers, and so do the disciples of the Pharisees, but yours eat and drink.' And Jesus said to them 'Can you make wedding guests fast while the bridegroom is with them?'" (Lk 5:33-34).

For the disciples, the presence of Jesus means freedom from fasting and mourning. Jesus does not limit table fellowship to his own followers but extends it to his contemporaries. When Jesus addresses the crowds, he compares them to sullen children complaining in the market-place (Lk 7:31-35), and in this passage the difference between himself and John is highlighted:

John	*Jesus*
not eating bread	*eating*
not drinking wine	*drinking*
called "possessed"	*called "glutton and drunkard;*
	friend of tax collectors and sinners"

Unlike the fasting John, the feasting Jesus eats with the rich and the poor, toll collectors and Zealots, Pharisees and sinners: he has a truly catholic taste for table companions, making him the most indiscriminate host in biblical tradition. His radical belief is that *unrestricted table fellowship is the best way of bringing salvation to people*, especially to those who are excluded from the Temple and the tables of the righteous. And since he believes that the kingdom of God looks like a magnificent feast for the legion of the unwanted, Jesus displays God's unique style in the present tense. Jesus wants the unwanted; he loves the unloved; he has a passion to break bread with broken people. The best way he shows all this is by his practice of welcoming sinners and eating with them, which is underlined by his message in the parables of The Great Feast, which celebrate indiscriminate table fellowship.

Salvation understood through the imagery of an inclusive banquet for *all peoples* is one that is celebrated in Jesus' own tradition: "On this mountain the Lord of hosts will make for all peoples a feast of fat things…And he will destroy on this mountain the covering that is cast over all peoples, the veil that is spread over all nations" (Is 25:6, 7). That image of the banquet for all peoples is given historical definition in the parables of Matthew and Luke: the messianic banquet is opened up to outsiders (the Gentiles) because those who were first chosen (the Jews) have themselves chosen to reject the invitations.

Matthew 22:1-14 (NRSV)

[1]Once more Jesus spoke to them in parables, saying: [2]"The kingdom of heaven may be compared to a king who gave a wedding banquet for his son. [3]He sent his slaves to call those who had been invited to the wedding banquet, but they would not come. [4]Again he sent other slaves, saying, 'Tell those who have been invited: Look, I have prepared my dinner, my oxen and my fat calves have been slaughtered, and everything is ready; come to the wedding banquet.' [5]But they made light of it and went away, one to his farm, another to his business, [6]while the rest seized his slaves, mistreated them, and killed them.

[7]"The king was enraged. He sent his troops, destroyed those murderers, and burned their city. [8]Then he said to his slaves, 'The wedding is ready, but those invited were not worthy. [9]Go therefore into the main streets, and invite everyone you find to the wedding banquet.' [10]Those slaves went out into the streets and gathered all whom they found, both good and bad; so the wedding hall was filled with guests.

[11]"But when the king came in to see the guests, he noticed a man there who was not wearing a wedding robe, [12]and he said to him, 'Friend, how did you get in here without a wedding robe?' And he was speechless. [13]Then the king said to the attendants, 'Bind him hand and foot, and throw him into the outer darkness, where there will be weeping and gnashing of teeth.' [14]For many are called, but few are chosen."

Matthew's parable

Matthew places this parable as a teaching in the last week of Jesus' life. Jesus has already entered Jerusalem, expelled the traffickers from the Temple, and is involved in controversy with the Jewish leaders – the chief priests and the elders of the people – about his own authority (21:23). Jesus counter-attacks with three parables:

> The Two Sons
> The Wicked Tenants
> The Great Banquet

The arrangement is clearly Matthew's own – Mark and Luke have only the parable of The Talents in the equivalent setting – and Matthew's setting of conflict with the religious leaders will, inevitably, largely determine the interpretation.

Matthew's host is a king; the occasion for the feast is the wedding celebration of his son. The king's slaves call the guests who have been invited to attend the feast, but they now bluntly refuse the royal summons. The king responds to this rejection by a new embassy of slaves, who carry their master's plea that the food is all prepared and the cattle slaughtered. The guests, however, remain stubborn in their refusal: one goes off to his field, another to his business, while the remainder manhandle and murder the king's slaves. Why wedding guests should suddenly turn to murder is not explained, but that absurdity is followed by another when the furious king organises a punitive expedition to kill the murderers and burn down their town. Meanwhile, the roast oxen, which by now must look like the burnt town, await attention. As the guests were stubborn in their refusal, the king is equally stubborn in his determination to have wedding guests. A third embassy is now sent out for new candidates, this time people from the streets of the town that has just been burnt. The good and the bad are brought in until the wedding hall is filled with guests.

The absurdities of the story are further magnified when the king complains that one of the new arrivals from the burnt town – one lucky to survive incineration – is not dressed suitably for a wedding, a reproach that would appear, were the consequences not so tragic, somewhat comical. The unlucky survivor is now thrown out into the dark, with his hands and feet bound.

Matthew's parable makes little sense in its present form: even fiction has to obey some laws of narrative logic if it is to invite the reader or listener into its world of story. It repeats the major themes of the parable preceding it, The Wicked Tenants: there the tenants beat or kill the slaves and murder the son because the emissaries all come with an unwelcome demand for fruit from the vineyard. The owner will respond by putting the slaves to death, "and let out the vineyard to other tenants who will give him fruit in their seasons" (Mt 21:41). That foundational story, whereby Judaism is condemned and Christianity authorised, is repeated in The Great Banquet. Both parables strain to explain the identity and authority of the new Christian community, what J. Drury calls "the fundamental Christian historical myth".[1] While Matthew's Great Feast, considered by itself, strains probability, it does, however, make sense as a coded history of the early Christian story. As allegory the figures can be interpreted thus:

wedding feast	=	*messianic age*
king	=	*figure of God*
first emissaries	=	*the prophets of Israel*
second emissaries	=	*apostolic preachers*
the king's army	=	*the Roman army that besieged Jerusalem*
town destroyed	=	*Jerusalem in AD 70 (burned down)*
newly invited	=	*Gentiles*

In this interpretation Matthew has developed a parable about a feast into an allegory of the whole of salvation history, beginning with the first invitation by the prophets to the chosen people, through their rejection of the prophets and the apostles, to the destruction of the city of Jerusalem and the transfer of the original invitation to the Gentiles.

Matthew's conclusion, the rejection of the guest who has no wedding garment, is best seen as an independent parable which the evangelist has tagged on to his allegorical story – perhaps to balance the "good and bad alike" who come for the feast. As T.W. Manson has pointed out it is similar to a story told by R. Johanan ben Zakkai, who was teaching around AD 70.[2] The story goes something like this:

> Once upon a time a certain king invited his slaves for a great feast, but did not say what time it would begin. The wise adorned themselves and waited at the gate of the palace. They said, "There is no shortage in the palace, so the feast will begin at any time." The foolish ones went to their work. They said: "There is no feast

without preparation, so it will not happen soon." Suddenly the king announced that all was ready. The wise ones came into his presence, dressed for the feast. The foolish ones came into his presence wearing their working clothes. The king was pleased with the wise slaves and angry with the foolish ones. He said: "Let those who are dressed for the feast sit down and eat and drink. Let those who are not properly dressed look on."

This version serves to explain in passing that wedding garments are what they normally are the world over – people's best clothes, not some special garment supplied by the host. Also, the king's punishment seems appropriate to the offence: looking on at a banquet, letting your eyes taste what you are missing, is penalty enough for not coming prepared. In The Wedding Garment Matthew probably means to teach that the new Christian community, made up of bad and good alike, is itself under judgement as an imperfect church. The story, however, makes little sense attached to the parable of The Great Feast.

In writing The Great Feast in the way that he does and in making The Wedding Garment the conclusion of the story, Matthew loses the governing image of a generous host who will have dinner with anyone. Instead, the themes of vengeance and destruction dominate his narrative. What Matthew loses, Luke manages to retain in his version of the parable.

Luke 14:16-24 (NRSV)

[16]*Then Jesus said to him, "Someone gave a great dinner and invited many.* [17]*At the time for the dinner he sent his slave to say to those who had been invited, 'Come; for everything is ready now.'* [18]*But they all alike began to make excuses. The first said to him, 'I have bought a piece of land, and I must go out and see it; please accept my regrets.'* [19]*Another said, 'I have bought five yoke of oxen, and I am going to try them out; please accept my regrets.'* [20]*Another said, 'I have just been married, and therefore I cannot come.'* [21]*So the slave returned and reported this to his master.*

"Then the owner of the house became angry and said to his slave, 'Go out at once into the streets and lanes of the town and bring in the poor, the crippled, the blind, and the lame.' [22]*And the slave said, 'Sir, what you ordered has been done, and there is still room.'* [23]*Then the master said to the slave, 'Go out into the roads*

and lanes, and compel people to come in, so that my house may be filled. [24]For I tell you, none of those who were invited will taste my dinner.'"

Luke's parable

Although Luke, like Matthew, establishes a setting of conflict for this parable, Luke's editorial framework does not have the aura of finality about it of Jesus' last week on earth. Luke sets the scene at a sabbath dinner in the house of a leading Pharisee, where Jesus' table companions, lawyers and Pharisees, are watching him (14:1). Luke uses the setting of the dinner party to gather together a series of sayings by Jesus on the general theme of table fellowship.

The scene opens with Jesus healing a man with dropsy, then failing to provoke his table companions to enter a debate on healing on the sabbath. After changing the subject to a teaching on humility in choosing places at table, he challenges his host to invite the poor, the lame, the maimed and the blind when giving a dinner party. The host makes no reply to Jesus' challenge. A pious dinner-companion makes the remark: "Blessed is he who shall eat bread in the kingdom of God!" As G.B. Caird comments: "Such an exclamation could come only from one who is confident in the possession of his own invitation. The parable of Jesus shatters this complacency: the kingdom of God is not an other-worldly prospect to be contemplated with unctuous sentiment, but a present reality calling for immediate response; the banquet is now ready."[3] Following the pious outburst, Jesus counters with the parable of The Great Feast.

The similarities and differences between Matthew's royal wedding feast and Luke's banquet scene can be seen from the following tables.

MATTHEW	LUKE
a) Royal wedding feast celebrated by a king for his son	a) Great feast given by a man
b) Slaves sent to call the invited	b) Slave sent to call the invited
c) Response: refusal of guests	c) Response: all make excuses
d) More slaves sent: "Everything is now ready"	

e) Response:
    farm work
    business
    murder servants
	see new land
	    try pairs of oxen
	    stay with new wife

f) The king is furious: he sends out troops; murderers are destroyed; town is burned down	d) The man is furious
g) More slaves sent, to cross-roads, to collect "both good and bad"	e) Sends slave into streets for "the poor, maimed, blind and the lame"
Appendix: Rejection of man without the wedding-garment	f) Sends slave to open roads, "that my house may be filled"

Luke's host, though not a king, is a wealthy man who can afford to entertain his many friends with a banquet. The double invitation was a courtesy practised by the wealthy. The response to the first invitation determined the numbers to be catered for – thus the menu and the amount could be decided on the basis of how many agreed to attend. The second invitation, effectively a summons, followed on the completion of all the preparations: "Come, for all is now ready."

A last-minute refusal to attend a great banquet is discourteous in any culture, particularly when the refusal is supported only by lame excuses. While all the guests exempt themselves, Luke uses the folkloric threesome to explore how weak the excuses really are. The first to refuse says that he has bought a field and now wants to see it, which seems an inane way to purchase land, particularly in a country of limited land space where there is a growing number of landless tenants.

As K.E. Bailey comments: "No one buys a field in the Middle East without knowing every square foot of it like the palm of his hand. The springs, wells, stone walls, trees, paths, and anticipated rainfall are all well known long before a discussion of the purchase is even begun. Indeed these items must be known, for in the past they were carefully included in the contract."[4]

The second refuser says that he has bought five pairs of oxen and *now* wants to go and examine them. Again inspection follows the purchase. To buy five teams of oxen unseen and untested, when the whole point of buying *pairs* is to ensure that they can work yoked together, is simply ludicrous. Apart from that, to tell a host that your animals are more important than your word, that their dumb presence is more significant than his company, makes for undisguised insult.

Unlike the previous two, the bridegroom does not ask to be excused but declines to come without offering a reason: he has married a bride, presumably recently, and so cannot come to the banquet. Why this thought never struck him when he first agreed to attend is not explained. Some commentators point out that a newly married man was excused from going to war (Dt 20:7; 24:5); J.D. Derrett's argument that participation in war is envisaged following the banquet seems a strained attempt at harmonisation.[5] There is no hint of war in Luke's parable: to use Matthew's parable, which has a war but no bridegroom, with Luke's parable, which has a bridegroom but no war, is too contrived to make literary sense. If Luke had meant to make the bridegroom's excuse reasonable he would hardly have included the comprehensive exclusion of the original guests at the end of the parable.

When the slave reports back to his master that none of the original guests will be attending, no doubt detailing the insulting excuses, the master is naturally angry. But his anger does not lead him to cancel the banquet; the urgency is not for revenge but to stay with the original intention of celebrating a banquet. The host moves on, extending the invitation to those in the community who are normally overlooked: the poor, the maimed, the blind, and the lame. He moves from disappointment and anger to the surprise of graciousness. The banquet is still on, and the guest list is now open to anyone from the city's streets that chooses to come.

When the slave brings in the legion of the afflicted from the streets, there is still room at the tables. The host wants the empty places taken, to fulfil his desire that his house be filled with guests. The slave is sent out again, this time farther afield to places beyond the host's community, to the highways and hedges, to persuade those who linger there to come to the banquet. The separate embassies of the host – first to those invited, then to the outcasts in the streets (of the town) and finally to the highways and hedges (outside the town) – clearly imply Luke's view of salvation: "It was necessary that the word of God should be spoken first to you. Since you thrust it from you, and judge yourselves unworthy of eternal life, behold, we turn to the Gentiles" (Acts 13:46). The final comment of the parable asserts the obvious: that the first invited shall have no taste of the celebrations, for there will be no participation from a distance.

Two other versions

In the non-canonical *Gospel of Thomas* there is another version of The Great Feast, which J.D. Crossan and J. Fitzmyer, like a number of commentators, argue is more primitive than the versions found in Matthew and Luke.[6] A man (not a king) sends one slave to summon the guests to dinner. The slave goes to four guests with the announcement, "My master summons you," but each guest in turn excuses himself with a particular reason: the first has some merchants coming to see him and he has to give them orders; the second has just bought a house and is needed for the day; the third has promised a newly married friend to arrange the dinner for him; the fourth has just bought a village and must go to collect the rents. Three of the excuses reveal businessmen focused on their dealings. When the master hears the report, there is no word that he is angry or that his honour has been insulted. He sends out his slave with the charge: "Go out into the streets and bring in those whom you will find that they may eat my dinner. But buyers and sellers shall not come into the place of my Father."

There is no need to interpret this parable in an allegorical sense: it stands on its own as a warning against the rich and a caution against lives focused on business commitments; the businessmen and merchants are excluded. In *Thomas*'s parable the second invitation – the final in Luke's – is not fulfilled within the story: while the *exclusion* of those first invited is final, the *invitation* is left as unfulfilled future. This makes particular sense in Luke's presentation, since Jesus himself does not organise any mission to the Gentiles: that mission is unfulfilled future during the ministry of Jesus.

J. Jeremias argues that in the original form of the parable, however that could be reconstructed, "Jesus was making use of well-known story material, namely, the story of the rich tax-gatherer Bar Ma'jan and a poor scholar, which occurs in the Aramaic in the Palestinian Talmud."[7] A summary of the story could go something like this:

> Once upon a time two men lived in Ashkelon. They ate together, drank together, studied the Law together. The poor scholar died, and no one took notice of his funeral. The other, a rich tax collector, Bar Ma'jan by name, was given a splendid funeral when he died. Everyone stopped working in the city that day, since all the people wanted to accompany the body of Bar Ma'jan to its final resting-place. How could God be so unjust by allowing this to happen? Although Bar Ma'jan had not lived an upright life, he had done a single good deed; while doing it, death surprised him in the act. Since his good deed had not been cancelled by any further wicked deeds, God had to reward it, and this was shown in his splendid funeral. What was his good deed? He had arranged a banquet for the city councillors, but they all refused to come. So he gave orders that the poor should come and eat, so that the food should not be wasted.

As in the parables in Matthew, Luke, and *Thomas,* the first chosen all conspire to reject the invitation, an act that would inevitably bring dishonour on the host's house. Their rejection reverses the host's expectation of having a banquet with the people *he* has chosen – be it his friends or those he would like to impress and put in his debt. Bar Ma'jan does not cancel the dinner because the city fathers rebuff him; the banquet is celebrated, albeit with curious substitutes for the influential politicians. And although he seems more concerned about wasting food than offering surprise hospitality to the poor, the reversal does take place: the invited guests are absent and those originally overlooked are present.

Reflection
In all four versions the rejection by the first chosen leads to something new and unexpected because of the host's deliberate refusal to allow the guests' rebuff to be the last word in the story of his banquet. No feast is cancelled; the banquet goes ahead with a mixed crowd of surprised guests. The movement from rejection to graciousness is not an automatic one – it depends entirely on the host's outlook. It is *the host's outlook,* it seems to me, rather than the guests' refusal, that lies at

the heart of each story. His unyielding commitment to sharing the feast is the dynamic that provides the momentum in the parable and the teaching of the parable.

If you organise a dinner party for your friends, you naturally invite those whose company you enjoy and want to share, the people who will provide the mixture of magic and agreeable contrast needed for a good dinner party. But what happens when, after expressing their ready support for the idea, all your guests decide that they have better things to do and turn you down?

What happens when people react with studied indifference to all the preparations you have made, to say nothing about how you might feel? How do you respond to their choice not to come? How do you face the rejection that you inevitably feel in the face of such a public refusal?

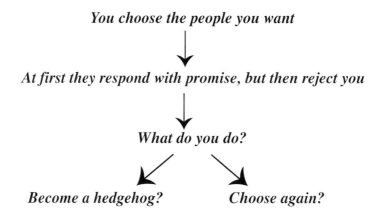

You choose the people you want

↓

At first they respond with promise, but then reject you

↓

What do you do?

↙ ↘

Become a hedgehog?   *Choose again?*

In rejection you can retire into your own protection, rather like the hedgehog. The hedgehog has its own answer to the world on its back. Over the years of evolutionary development, it has developed its own defence system: to escape from danger, it cannot run or fly or sting, but it can withdraw inside its own spiked world. It is protected inside its own enclosure; it does not depend on others; it is its own defence. We can all resort to that technique when we are rejected. As in Paul Muldoon's poem "Hedgehog":[8]

> The snail moves like a
> Hovercraft, held up by a
> Rubber cushion of itself,
> Sharing its secret

With the hedgehog. The hedgehog
Shares its secret with no one.
We say, *Hedgehog, come out
Of yourself and we will love you.*

*We mean no harm. We want
Only to listen to what
You have to say. We want
Your answers to our questions.*

The hedgehog gives nothing
Away, keeping itself to itself.
We wonder what a hedgehog
Has to hide, why it so distrusts.

We forget the god
Under this crown of thorns.
We forget that never again
Will a god trust in the world.

After a punishing experience of rejection we could all become like Muldoon's god, never again trusting the world. In all four stories of the banquet, however, particularly in Luke's parable, the host declines to retire inside his own hurt and rejection; instead, *he chooses again, moves out again, risks again*. Rather than providing a sad ending to the story, the rejection moves the narrative on, precisely because of the host's response. Confronted with an empty room and a banquet prepared, he stays fixed on his plan for feasting. When the chosen say no, there is a new urgency to ensure that the feast is enjoyed by others, which means that the host must choose again if he wants to fulfil his express desire "that my house may be filled". The feast is still on, but the faces are different around the table.

Given that the host wants the feast to be celebrated, the experience of rejection by the people he has chosen forces him to become more *catholic* in his choice of dinner companions. By force of circumstance he has to look for companionship where he normally never looks – beyond the circle of his cronies and friends to the legion of the overlooked. Rejection leads him to share table fellowship with people he would otherwise never have met.

That refusal to be tied down by those who say no, those who declare that they have better things to do than respond to your invitation, is one that Jesus lives out in his own ministry. Two brief examples will suffice. When Jesus is rejected by his own crowd in Nazareth he moves on, he chooses again, he offers himself and his message to a wider group of people. He does not remain stultified in the experience of rejection. And when he and his disciples enter a Samaritan village and are not welcomed by the people, Jesus refuses to take the advice of James and John when they suggest a holocaust as an appropriate pastoral response to rejection. After rebuking them, Jesus keeps going: "And they went on to another village" (Lk 9:56). There is a determination not to be diverted from the original mission or side-tracked because of people's meanness: "And wherever they do not receive you, when you leave that town shake off the dust from your feet as a testimony against them" (Lk 9:5).

In all this there is a stubborn refusal to be disabled by rejection alongside an equally stubborn commitment to keep the show on the road. Jesus continues to extend his message of good news and his ministry of table fellowship to those beyond the boundaries of social and religious approval. That brings him into open and hostile confrontation with other religious groups, but their criticism does not induce him to modify his mission statement: that the purpose of his ministry is to seek out and to save the lost (Lk 19:10). Jesus feasts with toll collectors and sinners in the belief that *feasting together* provides an opportunity to bring salvation to people. The parable of The Great Banquet celebrates the movement of Jesus' mission ever outwards, one that his followers will extend further in opening up table fellowship to the Gentiles.

A feast *not* shared: The Rich Man and Lazarus

The parable of The Rich Man and Lazarus offers us a counter image to the parable of The Great Feast, serving to illustrate what the messianic banquet is *not* – feasting apart from the afflicted. In this story there is no invitation, no mention of guests, no host anxious to share his table, no surprised banqueters. A rich man feasts inside his house while outside, at his gate, a beggar lies wanting and waiting. The reversal of fortune does not take place in life but in the afterlife.

Luke 16:19-31 (NRSV)

[19]*"There was a rich man who was dressed in purple and fine linen and who feasted sumptuously every day.* [20]*And at his gate lay a poor man named Lazarus, covered with sores,* [21]*who longed to satisfy his hunger with what fell from the rich man's table; even the dogs would come and lick his sores.* [22]*The poor man died and was carried away by the angels to be with Abraham. The rich man also died and was buried.*

[23]*"In Hades, where he was being tormented, he looked up and saw Abraham far away with Lazarus by his side.* [24]*He called out, 'Father Abraham, have mercy on me, and send Lazarus to dip the tip of his finger in water and cool my tongue; for I am in agony in these flames.'* [25]*But Abraham said, 'Child, remember that during your lifetime you received your good things, and Lazarus in like manner evil things; but now he is comforted here, and you are in agony.* [26]*Besides all this, between you and us a great chasm has been fixed, so that those who might want to pass from here to you cannot do so, and no one can cross from there to us.'* [27]*He said, 'Then, father, I beg you to send him to my father's house –* [28]*for I have five brothers – that he may warn them, so that they will not also come into this place of torment.'* [29]*Abraham replied, 'They have Moses and the prophets, they should listen to them.'* [30]*He said, 'No, father Abraham; but if someone goes to them from the dead, they will repent.'* [31]*He said to him, 'If they do not listen to Moses and the prophets, neither will they be convinced even if someone rises from the dead.'"*

The structure of the parable

The parable can be seen as a drama in two acts – the first act showing the rich man's luxurious lifestyle in contrast with the beggarly existence of Lazarus, the second act showing the finality of their reversal of fortunes in the next world. In both acts there is a boundary between the principal actors: the gate that marks the separation between the rich man and Lazarus in this life, and the gulf that exists between them in the next life. As the gate marks both the proximity and the separation between the two men in life, the gulf marks the distance and unalterable separation between them in the afterlife. Neither of the boundaries is crossed; both men remain separated.

Act One   the rich man in this world
                   _____
                   the poor man in this world

Act Two   the poor man in the next world
                   _____
                   the rich man in the next world

Act One: a divide that *can* be bridged in life

Inside the gate	*Outside the gate*
the rich man	*poor man, Lazarus*
dressed in purple and fine linen	*body covered in sores*
feasts magnificently every day	*longs to eat table scraps*
he dies	*he dies*
and is buried (given a proper funeral)	*and is carried off by angels*

Act Two: a divide that *cannot* be bridged in afterlife

Rich man in torment in Hades becomes beggar	*Lazarus in Abraham's bosom*
a) begs for pity and for Lazarus' service ⟶	*Abraham rejects plea:* *a fixed gulf now exists*
b) begs Lazarus be sent to warn his brothers ⟶	*Abraham rejects plea:* *Torah and Prophets enough*
c) begs for special treatment for family: *Lazarus' spirit will be listened to* ⟶	*Abraham rejects plea:* *it won't make any difference*

W. Vogels marks the difference by noting that the rich man moves from *having* to *not having and longing,* while Lazarus moves from *not having and longing* to *having and not longing*.[9] The reversal of fortunes is not justified in the parable by arguing that the rich man misused his wealth, or that Lazarus was destitute but pious. Abraham justifies the reversal not in moral terms but because of the stark inequality that existed between the two men in life: "Child, remember that during your lifetime you received your good things, and Lazarus in like manner evil things; but now he is comforted here, and you are in agony" (v.25). The radical inequality in life is reversed: it is now the turn of the rich man to suffer and of Lazarus to be consoled.

To some people, the reverse inequality in the afterlife may seem morally crude. But, as R. Bauckham comments, "If the theme of eschatological reversal were taken as a literal description of how God's justice will operate on earth it would be morally intolerable. However, if it is taken as a popular way of thinking which the parable uses to make a point, it can be seen as serving primarily to express and to highlight the intolerable injustice of the situation where one enjoys luxury and another suffers want. The motif of the eschatological reversal of fortunes for rich and poor surely belongs to the religious folklore of ordinary people, the poor. It is their hope in the justice of God against the injustice of this life as they experience it. Jesus in the parable takes up that perception, that hope and a popular way of expressing it."[10]

The drama of reversal

Not only does the parable express the popular hope that injustice will be reversed in the afterlife, it is surely critical of the social and economic forces that make for the original division between the rich man and the destitute Lazarus. The opening of the parable paints the difference in summary strokes. The rich man is clothed in purple, a very expensive dye from the shellfish murex, which was used only by royalty and the elite governing classes. Linen, an imported luxury item from Egypt, is also an indication of his wealth. He feasts as he dresses, sumptuously, and his feasting is a daily commitment rather than an exceptional event.

In sharp contrast, at the gate of the rich man's house, lies Lazarus (a name that means "God has helped"), one of society's expendables. The verb (the passive of *ballo*) indicates that he has been thrown down at the gate. His wardrobe is hardly magnificent – he is covered in sores – and he receives only the unwanted attention of stray dogs that feed off his ulcerated sores. His hopes are humble, longing, as he does, not to eat at the rich man's table but only to feed off the scraps from the dinner table. The scraps were probably the bread that guests used as napkins to wipe their fingers and then threw on the floor for the dogs. Lazarus hopes for what he has become: dog-food. He waits. His desire, however, remains unfulfilled.

After reporting the huge social gulf that exists between these two men, the first act concludes with reports on their death. When Lazarus dies, angels carry him to the bosom of Abraham; when the rich man dies, he receives a proper burial. The image of Abraham's bosom is clear: Lazarus is the honoured guest at the banquet of the patriarchs. *In the afterlife he is welcomed to a table fellowship he was so consistently denied in life.*

The second act shows the two actors enjoying/suffering a total reversal of fortune. The only explanation for the reversal is the social and economic division described in the first act. The rich man is in agony, and the flames that surround him represent the destruction of everything he valued. His fine clothes are gone; his feasting is finished; his fate is fixed. He now becomes the beggar, pleading for mercy from Abraham and asking that Lazarus be of service by cooling his tongue with water. In naming Lazarus, in expecting Lazarus to do his bidding, the rich man tells us that Lazarus was not one of the invisible poor, but known to him.

Abraham calls on the rich man to remember what happened in life so that he can understand its reversal in afterlife: *the second act develops the way it does because the first act developed the way it did.* Nothing more, nothing less. Following on this explanation, there is the revelation that the chasm between the one who was rich and the one who was destitute is fixed: just as there was no traffic between the poor at the gate and the rich at the table, neither is there traffic between the poor at the banquet and the rich in Hades.

The rich man goes on to plea-bargain for his own family, his concern noticeably limited to his five brothers who, granted the request, probably share the elite and exclusive lifestyle he once enjoyed. Abraham counters with the sufficiency of Moses and the prophets – their teaching is all the revelation that is needed. The rich man moves from pleading to arguing as he maintains that a visitor from the dead will ensure his brothers' repentance. Abraham is not convinced that people who are deaf to the voices of Moses and the prophets will become unaccountably alert to someone risen from the dead.

The fact that it is *Abraham* who welcomes the poor Lazarus and excludes the rich man is instructive, since the patriarch Abraham is presented in the tradition as a rich man himself (Gen 13:2), whose riches were interpreted as a sign of God's favour (Gen 14:13-24), someone who was buried with great honour (Gen 25:7-11). Given Abraham's favoured history, it might be expected that he would welcome the rich man to the heavenly banquet as someone who belonged to the same privileged world as himself. As W.R. Herzog comments: "The use of Abraham in the parable reinforces its purpose as codification. By selecting a figure whose value for legitimating the social order was great, Jesus increased the shock value of the representation while enlisting Abraham as advocate of the desperately poor."[11] The great patriarch is now the protector of the poor one, the stubborn excluder of the rich one: he is the ancient voice, older than the voices of Moses and the prophets, that teaches the rich the subversive values of Jesus' kingdom.

By refusing the rich man's brothers an apocalyptic revelation of the fate of the dead, Abraham brings the focus back to everyday life, where the rich live unaffected by the plight of the poor and the destitute. That is where the parable began, with the indefensible practice of a rich man feasting daily while a poor man lies destitute at his gate. That divisive scenario, it is argued, is already condemned in the Hebrew scriptures.

The message of the parable is clear: if the rich cannot *feast together* with the poor in this life, the poor shall feast without them in the kingdom.

---

[1] J. Drury, *The Parables in the Gospel* (London: SPCK, 1985) p.97

[2] T.W. Manson, *The Sayings of Jesus* (London: SCM, 1977) p.226. See also J. Jeremias, *The Parables of Jesus,* p.188

[3] G.B. Caird, *Saint Luke* (Middlesex: Penguin, 1963) p.177

[4] K.E. Bailey, *Through Peasant Eyes* (Grand Rapids: Eerdmans, 1980) p.95

[5] J.D. Derrett, *Law in the New Testament* (London: DLT, 1970) pp.126-155

[6] J.D. Crossan, *In Parables: the Challenge of the Historical Jesus* (New York: Harper & Row, 1973) pp.72-73; J.A. Fitzmyer, *The Gospel according to Luke X-XXIV* (New York: Doubleday, 1985) pp.1050-1052

[7] J. Jeremias, *The Parables of Jesus* p.178

[8] P. Muldoon, *Selected Poems 1968-1983* (London: Faber & Faber, 1986) p.8

[9] W. Vogels, "Having or Longing: A Semiotic Analysis of Luke 16:19-31" in *Église et Théologie* 20 (1989) pp.43-45

[10] R. Bauckham, "The Rich Man and Lazarus: the Parable and the Parallels" in *New Testament Studies* 37 (1991) p.233

[11] W.R. Herzog, *Parables as Subversive Speech*, p.130

Masters and slaves

The parable of The Talents (Mt 25:14-30) and the parable of The Pounds (Lk19:12-27) offer the modern reader a glimpse into the relationship between masters and slaves in the ancient world, between those who legally owned other human beings as property and those whose livelihood and future depended utterly on the approval of their respective owners. The Greek term *doulos* is properly translated as "slave" (not "servant" as in some translations); the word "slave" captures the complete subordination of the individual to the one who owns them. In Roman law the master's total legal control over his slave included the power over life and death.[1] In Hebrew law the premeditated killing of a slave was considered a crime, although no punishment is stipulated in the text (Ex 21:20).

The Hebrew law makes a distinction between slaves of Hebrew and foreign descent. Hebrews who were debtor slaves could be held in slavery for only six years, when they were to be set free (Ex 21:2; Dt 15:12; Jer 34:14). A Hebrew who sold himself to another Hebrew should have the status of a hired workman and after six years be returned to his family; if a Hebrew sold himself to a foreigner, the owner was obliged to set him free as soon as he or his relatives could pay for his redemption (Lev 25:39-41). One of the provisions for the Sabbatical Year legislation called for the release of all slaves at the beginning of the seventh year (Ex 21:2; Dt 15:12-14). It is difficult to assess, however, how strictly the laws regarding slavery were observed.

Writing about slavery in the Greco-Roman world, S.S. Bartchy argues that knowledge of slavery practised in the New World in the seventeenth to the nineteenth century has hindered a historical understanding of social economic life in the Mediterranean world of the first century: "Central features that distinguish 1st century slavery from that practised in the New World are the following: racial factors played no role; education was greatly encouraged (some slaves were better educated than their owners) and enhanced a slave's value; many slaves carried out sensitive and highly responsible social functions; slaves could own property (as well as other slaves!); their religious and cultural traditions were the same as those of the freeborn; no laws prohibited the public assembly of slaves; and (perhaps above all) the majority of urban and domestic slaves could legitimately anticipate being emancipated by the age of 30."[2] That emancipation, it has to be said, was not legally guaranteed but dependent on the good will of the slave's owner; for those who had been enslaved as convicted criminals, however, there was no hope of freedom.

Before the first century AD the Mediterranean world was supplied with slaves from prisoners of war and those kidnapped by pirates. After the death of Caesar Augustus, when the great wars of conquest came to an end, the primary source for slaves were the children of women in slavery. Although it sounds peculiar to modern ears, many people sold themselves into slavery not only to pay debts but also to advance their social position (especially where Roman citizenship was conferred on a slave released by a Roman owner). People became slaves to obtain secure jobs, and to avoid the perilous existence of destitute, freeborn people. Thus Paul admonishes the Christian Corinthians: "You were bought with a price; do not becomes slaves of men" (1 Cor 7:23). Although people could be legally termed as slaves, they could also enjoy social status and responsibility: K. Hopkins mentions "doctors, teachers, writers, accountants, agents, bailiffs, overseers, secretaries, and sea-captains".[3]

When the parables mention "slaves", they are focusing not on the social position or responsibility of the slaves but on their legal position as wholly subject to a master. Slaves were not distinguished by their dress, their race, their religion, or their lifestyle: many of the jobs they held could have easily been held by freeborn people, so it was not easy to determine who exactly they were. The fact that the parables focus on their position as *slaves*, however important their social status or responsibility, is significant for the dynamic of the story.

The owners of the slaves belonged to the elite class of landowners. At the time of Jesus, Palestine was a small client kingdom of the Roman Empire. The rulers (a Roman procurator governing the imperial province of Judea, Samaria, and Idumea; Herod Antipas, tetrarch of Galilee and Perea; Philip, tetrarch of territories to the north and east of Galilee) and their families could not, obviously, guarantee their own position from among their own ranks. They were assisted by a governing class, which needed a whole host of bureaucrats and retainers to maintain the position both of the ruler and themselves, guarantee their security, and advance their financial standing. First-century Palestine was a typical agrarian society ruled by an aristocratic elite, and it might be useful as background to the parables to note G. Lenski's representation of the relationship among classes in agrarian societies (Figure 1).[4]

Figure 1

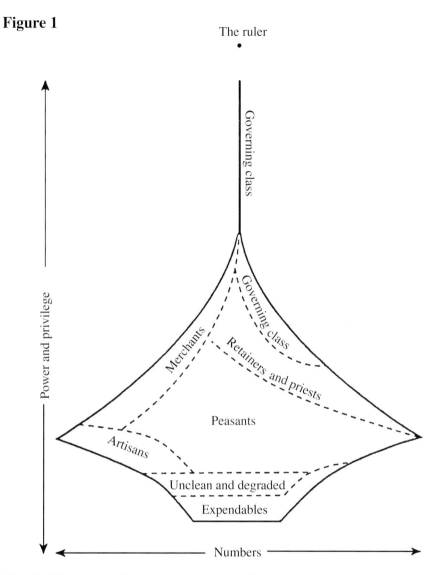

The buffer group between the governing class and the peasants were the retainers, who played the vital role of implementing the policies of their masters. As W.R. Herzog comments: "Usually their salaries were low, but they also garnered wealth through 'honest graft.' The rewards available at the highest level of the bureaucracy were lucrative, but the price paid by bureaucrats for doing their work, at any level of the system, was also high, because bureaucratic retainers absorbed the hostility directed at the invisible elites. Indeed, one of their roles was to shield elites from popular violence and resentment directed against the exploitative and oppressive policies of the elites. . . Their most important functions were to identify the surplus produced by the peasants, artisans and other villagers and to transfer it to the control of the ruler. They were the agents of redistribution in the economy."[5] Priests were numbered among the retainer class as they were in the service of the Temple elite.

Merchants and traders were usually of relatively low rank or status on the social scale, but their power and prestige – gained as a result of wealth from their trade – might be great. Most merchants probably emerged from the lower classes, but as Lenski notes, "in virtually every mature agrarian society, merchants managed to acquire a considerable portion of the wealth, and in a few instances a measure of political power as well".[6] The vast majority of the population, between 70 and 80 per cent, were peasants who worked on the land and lived in the towns and villages. Although their labour generated the wealth of an agrarian society, the peasants had to struggle hard to answer the subsistence needs of their own families, pay their rents and taxes and tithes, and ensure they had sufficient resources to cover failing crops.

Artisans, such as carpenters, stonemasons and potters, had no security but their trade and thus were wholly dependent on employment. (It might be worth noting in passing that with the rebuilding of Sepphoris,[7] the administrative capital of Galilee, which was about an hour's walk from Nazareth, and the building of the new city of Tiberias on the western shore of the Sea of Galilee, there was much demand for Galilean artisans during the reign of Herod Antipas.) Those Lenski identifies as "unclean and degraded" were those whose work was considered unclean by the population – such as donkey-peddlers and prostitutes. At the bottom of the heap are the "expendables" – those who had no security from land, employment or family, the legion of the unemployed that survived as beggars or itinerant day labourers, or those who took to crime as a means of survival.

In contrast to the rural countryside dotted by villages and towns, the cities were the centres of wealth, trade and industry; they were controlled by councils made up of Greek-speaking landowners and officials. Many of the cities of Palestine bore names whose roots were Greek or Latin: Appolonia, Tiberias, Caesarea Philippi, Julias. In most cities the population would have been predominately Gentile. The cities enjoyed a considerable measure of independence, provided they paid tribute and co-operated with the controlling power. The councils ruling the cities had the freedom to make their own laws, which also applied to the surrounding rural areas: this political power gave the rich landowners the opportunity to ensure hereditary rights to their estates and villages, and especially the land they acquired in repayments for unpaid loans.

Absentee landlords, like the figures in both parables, would spend a significant portion of their time not only in the city councils but also travelling abroad, to ensure that their base of power and privilege could be extended.

Luke 19:11-27 (NRSV)

[11]*As they were listening to this, he went on to tell a parable, because he was near to Jerusalem, and because they supposed that the kingdom of God was to appear immediately.* [12]*So he said, "A nobleman went to a distant country to get royal power for himself and then return.* [13]*He summoned ten of his slaves, and gave them ten pounds, and said to them, 'Do business with these until I come back.'* [14]*But the citizens of his country hated him and sent a delegation after him, saying, 'We do not want this man to rule over us.'*

[15]*"When he returned, having received royal power, he ordered these slaves, to whom he had given the money, to be summoned so that he might find out what they had gained by trading.* [16]*The first came forward and said, 'Lord, your pound has made ten more pounds.'* [17]*He said to him, 'Well done, good slave! Because you have been trustworthy in a very small thing, take charge of ten cities.'* [18]*Then the second came, saying, 'Lord, your pound has made five pounds.'* [19]*He said to him, 'And you, rule over five cities.'*

[20]*"Then the other came, saying, 'Lord, here is your pound. I wrapped it up in a piece of cloth,* [21]*for I was afraid of you, because you are a harsh man; you take what you did not deposit, and reap what you did not sow.'* [22]*He said to him, 'I will judge you by your own words, you wicked slave! You knew, did you, that I was a harsh man, taking what I did not deposit and reaping what I did not sow?* [23]*Why then did you not put my money into the bank? Then when I returned, I could have collected it with interest.'* [24]*He said to the bystanders, 'Take the pound from him and give it to the one who has ten pounds.'* [25]*(And they said to him, 'Lord, he has ten pounds!')* [26]*'I tell you, to all those who have, more will be given; but from those who have nothing, even what they have will be taken away.* [27]*But as for these enemies of mine who did not want me to be king over them – bring them here and slaughter them in my presence.'"*

Luke's parable

The context Luke provides for this parable is Jesus' final teaching on the journey to Jerusalem. The parable is placed after Jesus' dinner at the house of Zacchaeus and before his entry into the city of Jerusalem. Luke tells us that Jesus recounts the parable to refute false expectations that the kingdom of God is going to show itself immediately. As it is written Luke's text seems to be a conflation of two parables (the parable of The Throne Claimant and the parable of The Pounds) which could stand independently of each other. In the following summary of Luke's text I have outlined the parable of The Throne Claimant in bold italic, showing how it can be read by itself.

A nobleman travels to a far country to increase his power by securing the title of king. Summoning his slaves he gives ten of them the same amount each, ten pounds, charging them to do business with his money. *His citizens hate him and have no wish to be ruled by him, so they send representatives to oppose his claim, but he does return as king. On his return* he summons his slaves to discover what gains they have made in his absence. The first slave, who has made ten pounds, is commended and rewarded with the charge of ten cities. The second slave, who has made five pounds, is commended and rewarded with the rule of five cities. The third slave, who has refused to make his master richer in his absence, returns the pound, explaining that he was afraid not only of his master's harshness but also of his master's habitual theft: the master takes what does not belong to him and carries off the produce of other people's farming. The king calls this slave wicked, although he does not disagree with his slave's estimation of him. After taking the pound from the third slave and giving it to the first slave, *the king orders the execution of those who opposed his kingship.*

The story of a man of noble birth travelling abroad to acquire for himself the title of king is one that has an interesting historical parallel in Archelaus, the eldest son and successor of Herod the Great. In the final version of his will Herod named Archelaus as principal heir to his kingdom.[8] Archelaus refrained from using the royal title "king" – one that could be bestowed only by Augustus – but was soon faced with demands for the reduction and abolition of taxes, the release of prisoners, and the replacement of the high priest appointed by his father. In order to settle the serious unrest that followed, Archelaus ordered his cavalry into the Temple precincts: they killed 3,000 Jews in a bloodthirsty purge.[9]

Archelaus sailed to Rome to petition Augustus for his father's throne. During his absence, the civil unrest developed into widespread rebellion. The Roman governor of Syria, Varus, restored order and also gave permission for a Jewish delegation to sail to Rome to oppose the claim of Archelaus: they requested that Judea be annexed and ruled directly from Rome.[10] Augustus compromised: he divided Herod's property, probably to ensure the future of Herod's dependants and go some way to satisfy the Jewish delegation that demanded abolition of the monarchy. He awarded the title of ethnarch to Archelaus, with the territories of Judea, Samaria and Idumea, together with a number of cities, including Jerusalem. Antipas was confirmed as tetrarch of Galilee and Perea, and Philip, tetrarch of Gaulanitis, Trachonitis, Batanea and Paneas.

Although Archelaus did not gain the title king, it is interesting to note that Josephus calls him "king" – which might be a popular indication of the scope of Archelaus' power. On his return he exacted a cruel revenge on his opponents. Speaking of Archelaus' tyrannical rule, Josephus notes how Archelaus, "remembering past differences, behaved savagely not only towards Jews but also towards the Samaritans".[11] He remained in office only ten years, until AD 6. Because of Archelaus' stubborn commitment to violence as his principal form of government, Augustus summoned the ethnarch to Rome, exiled him to Vienne in Gaul, and appointed a Roman procurator to govern his territories.

It is highly probable that the story of Archelaus' brutal reign formed the background for the parable of The Throne Claimant. One of the peculiar advantages of Luke's conflation is that it makes it difficult, though not impossible given the *context*, for the reader to idealise the king as a figure for God. Luke's literary context – the delay of the parousia – tends to lead the reader to interpret the parable as a warning that the intervening period will be a time of testing. As J. Jeremias observed: "Luke, then, would seem to have interpreted the nobleman who received a kingdom and demanded a reckoning from his servants on his return, as the Son of Man departing to heaven and returning to judgement. But Luke is certainly wrong. For it is hardly conceivable that Jesus would have compared himself, either with a man 'who drew out where he had not paid in, and reaped where he had not sown,' that is, a rapacious man, heedlessly intent on his own profit: or with a brutal oriental despot, gloating over the sight of his enemies slaughtered before his eyes."[12]

If the reader identifies the king as a figure of God, inevitably the third slave will be seen as wicked and lazy. But if the reader resists ascribing moral superiority to the one who is economically powerful and has total control over his subjects, then the parable is allowed to speak for itself and we can follow its clues about the different characters involved in the drama. The central question is: Was the third slave right in refusing to collaborate further in making his rich master richer? I will leave that question until we look at Matthew's parable.

Matthew 25:14-30 (NRSV)

[14] *"For it is as if a man, going on a journey, summoned his slaves and entrusted his property to them;* [15] *to one he gave five talents, to another two, to another one, to each according to his ability. Then he went away.* [16] *The one who had received the five talents went off at once and traded with them, and made five more talents.* [17] *In the same way, the one who had the two talents made two more talents.* [18] *But the one who had received the one talent went off and dug a hole in the ground and hid his master's money.*

[19] *"After a long time the master of those slaves came and settled accounts with them.* [20] *Then the one who had received the five talents came forward, bringing five more talents, saying, 'Master, you handed over to me five talents; see, I have made five more talents.'* [21] *His master said to him, 'Well done, good and trustworthy slave; you have been trustworthy in a few things, I will put you in charge of many things; enter into the joy of your master.'* [22] *And the one with the two talents also came forward, saying, 'Master, you handed over to me two talents; see, I have made two more talents.'* [23] *His master said to him, 'Well done, good and trustworthy slave; you have been trustworthy in a few things, I will put you in charge of many things; enter into the joy of your master.'*

[24] *"Then the one who had received the one talent also came forward, saying, 'Master, I knew that you were a harsh man, reaping where you did not sow, and gathering where you did not scatter seed;* [25] *so I was afraid, and I went and hid your talent in the ground. Here you have what is yours.'* [26] *But his master replied, 'You wicked and lazy slave! You knew, did you, that I reap where I did not sow, and gather where I did not scatter?* [27] *Then you ought to have invested my money with the bankers, and on my return I would have received what was my own with interest.* [28] *So take the talent from him, and give it to the one with the ten talents.* [29] *For to all those who have, more will be given, and they will have an abundance; but from those who have nothing, even what they have will be taken away.* [30] *As for this worthless slave, throw him into the outer darkness, where there will be weeping and gnashing of teeth.'"*

Masters and stewards

Matthew, like Luke, sets the drama in the household of a rich man who has a number of slaves who act as his retainers or stewards. While Luke's owner is a rich nobleman who later becomes the ultimate ruler, Matthew's character is a man whose power and riches become quickly evident as the story develops. Both men are masters of great households, whose influence is not confined to their domestic base.

In an agrarian society the masters of the great households were the principal landowners by whom the wealth of the land was controlled. As landed proprietors, they had been able to acquire and to increase vast domains; as far back as Isaiah they had attracted the curse, "Ah, you who join house to house, and field to field, until there is room for no one but you, and you are left to live alone in the midst of the land!" (Is 5:8). They joined field to field not just to amass land but, more importantly, to control which crops were grown: clearly, a harvest of grapes from a large vineyard would make more money as a luxury item than a few fields of barley. As the rich landowners could afford to specialise in luxury crops, most peasant farmers, with small plots of land, had space to grow only what they needed for their family's subsistence. As H. Daniel-Rops comments: "The Palestinian economy was still somewhat primitive, and each farm had a tendency to try to produce everything it needed."[13]

The masters of the great households also made up the governing elite in the city councils, thereby controlling not only the urban domain but also the lands surrounding the city. Thus Nazareth, for example, a village of around 150 inhabitants, was within the authority of the city council of Sepphoris. The business of politics was concentrated on the *polis* (city) and exercised only by those who belonged to the ruling families. This undisturbed access to power made it easy for the land-owning elite to exploit their position over the vast majority of the voiceless. In this light it is worth noting G. de Sainte Croix's observation on class:

> Class, then, essentially a relationship, is above all the collective social expression of the fact of exploitation (and of course of resistance to it): the division of society into economic classes is in its very nature the way in which exploitation is effected, with the propertied classes living off the non-propertied. I admit that in my use of it the word "exploitation" often tends to take on a pejorative

colouring; but essentially it is a "value-free" expression, signifying merely that a propertied class is freed from the labour of production through its ability to maintain itself out of a surplus exacted from the primitive producers, whether by compulsion or by persuasion or (in most cases) by a mixture of the two.[14]

While the rich, propertied class had a staff of retainers, depending on the size of their households – stewards, tutors, scribal accountants, etc. – the key figures in the financial advancement of the household were the stewards. The landed gentry had no need to persuade their stewards to make them richer by acquiring more land: that was their principal function in an agrarian society where wealth was based on land. As T. Carney comments, wealth was generated by a "seize or squeeze" principle: "Capital was formed in antiquity by taking it from someone else . . . or as taxes squeezed out of a toiling peasant population."[15] In both parables how the slave-stewards manage to "seize or squeeze" is left to their own devices. As slaves (*douloi*) they are wholly subject to their master's authority; as stewards, while enjoying the privileged status and authority that come from being attached to their master's household, they are compelled to increase their master's wealth. If they fail to do that, they become disposable property – which happens to one of them in the parable.

The structure of Matthew's parable

Scene 1: The challenge
a) Before going abroad, the master hands over his wealth to his slaves
b) He distributes his money (talents) in proportion to the slave's *dynamis*
    1st slave receives 5 talents; 2nd slave: 2 talents; 3rd slave: 1 talent
c) Then the master leaves them, without instructions, to make him richer

Scene 2: The response
a) 1st slave promptly "trades" 5 talents and makes 5 more
b) 2nd slave makes 2 more talents in the same way
c) 3rd slave goes off and digs a hole and hides his master's money

Scene 3: The reckoning
a) When the master returns he goes through the accounts with his slaves
b) *1st slave*: "You handed over to me 5 talents; see, I have made 5 more"
    Master: "Well done, good and trustworthy slave; you have been
                trustworthy... I will put you in charge of greater things . . ."
c) *2nd slave*: "You handed over to me 2 talents; see, I have made 2 more"
    Master: "Well done, good and trustworthy slave; you have been
                trustworthy… I will put you in charge of many things . . ."
d) *3rd slave*: "I knew you were harsh man, reaping where you did not sow,
                and gathering where you did not scatter seed; so I was
                afraid...and hid your talent"
    Master: "You wicked and lazy slave! You knew . . . Take talent from
                him . . . For all who have more will be given . . . As for this
                worthless slave, throw him into the outer darkness . . ."

The two profiteers

In Matthew's parable the master is going abroad on a business venture and wants to ensure that his money generates more money during his absence. He hands over (*paradidomi*) the capital he does not immediately require and divides it among three of his stewards according to the *dynamis* of each one, that is, according to their power or status in the household. The power or status of a steward reflected his proven ability to increase his master's wealth. The cash amounts are in talents: originally a measure of weight, the talent became the highest single unit of currency in the Hellenistic world. (The word passed into the English language in the Middle Ages as a synonym for a person's native ability or natural endowments, but here it refers only to money.) The approximate ratios are: 100 denarii = 1 mina (pound); 6,000 denarii = 1 talent. By any standards, the rich master's liquid assets are considerable, yet he can speak of them as trifling sums and promise far more to his successful stewards (verses 21, 23).

What is left unstated in the parable is how the first two stewards make 100 per cent profit, but this would have been unnecessary information to Jesus' original listeners. As T. Carney has indicated, the principal means by which rich landowners increased their wealth in an agrarian society was by following the imperative "seize or squeeze". This exploitation of peasant farmers was easily done when there was crop failure: if the farmers needed loans, the only collateral they could offer was their land. If they failed to honour the repayment of the loan and the exorbitant interest, the inevitable foreclosure followed.

The landed gentry's expropriation of peasant land brought them the obvious benefit of extending their base for cash crops, particularly the kind that could be sold or exported to a luxury market, while reducing another farmer to a dependant status, either as a tenant or a day labourer. The stewards are the principal collaborators in their master's exploitative ways. Exploited themselves as slaves, the stewards in the parables are called on to become like their master and grow richer through taking unfair advantage of less fortunate people. Just as the master admits that his own lucrative business is based on taking what does not belong to him – "I reap where I did not sow, and gather where I did not scatter" – he presumes that his stewards will imitate his aggressive tactics.

In making a profit for their master – exactly double in each case – the first two stewards would also have made a profit for themselves. Although the master is gone for a long time, the first two stewards go to work immediately: when they make their master a generous profit, they can dedicate their energies to securing their own financial gain. Provided stewards secured a generous profit margin for their master, their "honest graft" was regarded as an acceptable part of business transactions.

I find it interesting to note that at the beginning of the parable Matthew states that the man (*anthropos*) goes away, but from verse 19, when the reckoning begins, the man is now called lord (*kyrios*) of the slaves and addressed as *kyrie* by the three slaves. As their lord, the rich man commends his first two stewards in turn: "Well done, good and trustworthy slave . . ." and rewards them by promotion to a more powerful position in his bureaucracy of exploitation. Notwithstanding the master's offer of promotion, his speech reminds his two listeners that their basic relationship (lord/slave, patron/client) has not changed: they remain *his* slaves and they are privileged to share in *his* joy, literally "the joy of the lord of you". Whatever changes are made, there are no changes in his lordship's possessive pronouns.

What makes these stewards good in the eyes of their rich lord? His designation of them as "good and trustworthy" reflects that his morality is informed by his economics: he praises his stewards because they have succeeded in making him considerably richer, just as he will condemn his third steward as wicked because he has failed to make him any profit. In rewarding the two profiteers with more power he is ensuring that they will remain as he wants them: dependent slaves improving their exploitive arts on behalf of their lord. While the stewards' promotion will doubtless give them even better opportunities to enrich themselves, it also deepens their obligation to their master. In a world of patronage, who they are is what their lord has made them; whatever they are, they owe to him.

The speeches we have heard so far – the two stewards' speeches focusing on individual success and profit and the master's two responses of praise and promotion – serve to disguise the brutal reality that lies behind all their combined profit-making schemes. There is no word about the losers, the nameless peasants who account for the named profits. Their story of loss goes unrecognised in the rhetoric of the winners.

The third slave

The third slave, who receives more extended treatment than the other two slaves together, is clearly the focus of the parable. Compared with the brief, formal speeches of his fellow stewards, the third steward's account is detailed and confrontational. He first identifies his lord as a harsh man whose style of profiteering is indistinguishable from theft: a man who takes what does not belong to him and benefits from the labour of others. There is nothing shocking in the content of this description, for it is no secret how rich landowners make money, and the master will not correct it. T.W. Manson, even though he believes the third slave to be wrong, still makes the point: "The master makes no attempt to rebut the charge. As between master and slave the statement of the case is correct. That *is* the situation. The slave works and the master takes the result of his labours."[16] What is shocking in an honour/shame culture is that the master's exploitative leadership is denounced publicly and that the denunciation is made by one of his own slaves.

The third steward explains that the knowledge of his master's way of making money out of depriving others made him afraid, leading him to hide the talent in the ground. Without further comment, he offers to restore intact the amount the master gave him.

The master calls this unprofitable slave "wicked and lazy" for the same reason that he called the other two "good and trustworthy": the moral adjectives reflect only ability or inability to make money. He does not dispute his slave's summary of him. As Richard Ford notes: "To realise that ethical issues are at stake, one has only to contemplate the slave-master's 'moral outrage.' This man's contempt may be provoked not only by his greed but also by his accurate suspicion that this last slave has indeed read him out for who he is."[17] The master's interest, however, is not diverted from his unyielding attachment to profit. So committed is he to the profit motive that he finds it incomprehensible that his slave, even in a state of fear, should have failed to gain him interest by depositing the money with the bankers. He is wholly uninterested in his slave's fear: the master believes naively that the primary urge to make a profit must overshadow any fear, even if that fear has its base in the exploitation of other people.

The master will not give this steward a second opportunity. Refusing to receive the talent from the third steward, the master orders that it be taken from him and given to the most productive steward. This action, transferring the one talent to the hands of the most profitable steward, sets the scene for a classic formulation of exploitative business practice: "For to all those who have, more will be given, and they will have an abundance; but from those who have nothing, even what they have will be taken away." While this is the working philosophy of the lord of the slaves and his collaborating stewards, it is hardly a reflection of the values of Jesus.

The final verse, where the master condemns his "worthless slave" to the outer darkness, may be Matthew's editorial addition, although it is consistent with the final expulsion of a slave who has become a useless object in his master's household. An unprofitable slave who has grown to disapprove of his master's greed and refuses to follow the profiteer's script is dumped on the scrap-heap of life. That is a dramatic lesson to any others that might think of opposing the economy of the exploiter.

Expelling untrustworthy slaves from the household was one way of "emancipating" them. As S.S. Bartchy observes: "An owner who feared that the courts might force his slaves under torture (the standard procedure) to reveal 'too much' about the owner's activities could emancipate the slaves in question; ex-slaves could only be required to testify against their patrons in cases involving treason."[18] Expulsion would mean, of course, that no other household would risk employing such a non-conformist: "emancipation" through expulsion was social death, a point that the final verse captures dramatically.

Reflection

The third slave may be regarded as a lazy fool for jeopardising his prospects, which is the dominant view among Western interpreters. Or he may be looked upon as a moral hero for daring to break out of the circle of exploitation. In order to win the original trust of his master, he must have been skilled as a steward: what made him change? The only reason we are given in the text is that he became fearful of his master's harshness in business dealings. Did this fear lead him to bury the talent as a way of limiting what he feared, his master's power? By taking it out of circulation, by making it unavailable to be used for usurious loans, the third steward's action could be interpreted in a positive light.

The dominant view is that the burial of the talent is the action of a fearful, lazy steward who can no longer be bothered with his responsibilities. Laziness, it has to be said, hardly warrants a parable to disclose its destructive effects; it can be condemned openly without the need of encoding it in parabolic form. Is something else being encoded in the parable – the practice of exploitation sanctioned by tradition, one that can be broken only when the exploiters and their collaborators cease lording it over others and using them simply for profit?

R. Rohrbaugh argues that "Jesus' peasant hearers would almost certainly have assumed (the parable) was a warning to the rich about their exploitation of the weak."[19] This view is dependent on freeing the parable from the context provided by both Matthew and Luke, looking at the parable in the light of social inequities in first-century Palestine, and also, I believe, interpreting the parable in a way that is consistent with Jesus' own teaching. Given Jesus' instruction to his disciples on the dangers of riches (e.g. Mt 19:23-26), the abuse of authority (e.g. Mt 19:25-28), and respect for the little ones (e.g. Mt 18:1-7) the parable's interpretation as a coded critique of rich landowners' abuse of their economic power would seem more consistent with Jesus' own values.

The third slave is condemned for two reasons: he refuses to co-operate further in his rich master's habitual theft and he exposes and demystifies the corrupt way his master enriches himself and his household. Both of the slave's actions are laudable according to the values of Jesus, for the slave neither exploits nor steals, nor does he lend his silent support to the powerful who do both. He, not the rich landowner, is the spokesman of the parable's moral.

The third slave suffers not just the disapproval of the elite but total ostracism because of his dangerous activity. As we will see in the parable of The Pharisee and the Toll Collector, Jesus does in that parable what he does in life – he symbolically overthrows the system that supports its own mystified oppression. Jesus exposes and demystifies the old order of the Temple power and its supporters while he champions the outsider in the person of the toll collector. In acting like this, Jesus himself will pay the ultimate price for taking on the system he exposes: he will be dismissed by the power brokers of that same system into the ultimate outer darkness of death.

---

[1] See W.V. Harris, "The Roman Father's Power of Life and Death" in R.S. Bagnall and W.V. Harries (Eds.), *Studies in Roman Law in Memory of A. Arthur Schiller* (Leiden: Brill, 1986) pp.81-95

[2] S.S. Bartchy, "Slavery (Greco-Roman) in the New Testament" in *The Anchor Bible Dictionary* Vol 6 (New York: Doubleday, 1992) p.66

[3] K. Hopkins, *Conquerors and Slaves* (New York: Sociological Studies in Roman History 1, 1978) p.123

[4] G. Lenski, *Power and Privilege: A Theory of Social Stratification* (New York: McGraw-Hill, 1966) p.284; see also G. Lenski and J. Lenski, *Human Societies* (New York: McGraw-Hill,1974) pp.207-262

[5] W.R. Herzog, *Parables as Subversive Speech,* p.61

[6] G. Lenski, *Power and Privilege*, p.250

[7] Called by Josephus "the ornament of all Galilee" (*Jewish Wars* 2.5.11) and "the strongest city in Galilee" (*Antiquities* 18.27)

[8] Josephus, *Antiquities* 17.188-189

[9] Josephus, *Antiquities* 17.218

[10] Josephus, *Antiquities* 17.299-314

[11] Josephus, *Jewish War* 2.111

[12] J. Jeremias, *The Parables of Jesus,* pp.60-61

[13] H. Daniel-Rops, *Daily Life in the Time of Jesus* (Ann Arbor: Servant, 1980) p.235

[14] G.E. de Sainte Croix, "Karl Marx and the History of Classical Antiquity" in *Arethusa* 8 (1975) p.26

[15] T. Carney, *The Shape of the Past: Models and Antiquity* (Lawrence: Coronado Press, 1975) p.97

[16] T.W. Manson, *The Sayings of Jesus*, p.247

[17] R.Q. Ford, *The Parables of Jesus: Recovering the Art of Listening* (Minneapolis: Fortress Press, 1997) p.45

[18] S.S. Bartchy, "Slavery (Greco-Roman) in the New Testament", p.71

[19] R.L. Rohrbaugh, "A Peasant Reading of the Parable of the Talents/Pounds: A Text of Terror?" in *Biblical Theology Bulletin* 23 (1993) p.38

Matthew 20:1-16 (RSV)

[1]*"For the kingdom of heaven is like a householder who went out early in the morning to hire labourers for his vineyard.* [2]*After agreeing with the labourers for a denarius a day, he sent them into his vineyard.* [3]*And going out about the third hour he saw others standing idle in the market place;* [4]*and to them he said, 'You go into the vineyard too, and whatever is right I will give you.' So they went.* [5]*Going out again about the sixth hour and the ninth hour, he did the same.* [6]*And about the eleventh hour he went out and found others standing; and he said to them, 'Why do you stand here idle all day?'* [7]*They said to him, 'Because no one has hired us.' He said to them, 'You go into the vineyard too.'*

[8]*"And when evening came, the owner of the vineyard said to his steward, 'Call the labourers and pay them their wages, beginning with the last, up to the first.'* [9]*And when those hired about the eleventh hour came, each of them received a denarius.* [10]*Now when the first came, they thought they would receive more; but each of them also received a denarius.* [11]*And on receiving it they grumbled at the householder,* [12]*saying, 'These last worked only one hour, and you have made them equal to us who have borne the burden of the day and the scorching heat.'* [13]*But he replied to one of them, 'Friend, I am doing you no wrong; did you not agree with me for a denarius?* [14]*Take what belongs to you, and go; I choose to give to this last as I give to you.* [15]*Am I not allowed to do what I choose with what belongs to me? Or do you begrudge my generosity?'* [16]*So the last will be first, and the first last."*

Introduction

For many people, the parable of The Labourers in the Vineyard leaves them feeling somewhat confused and uncertain, not least because their secret sympathy might be for the first-hired labourers who express their hurt and disappointment at being paid the same as the last-hired labourers. The parable retains its power to disturb, even to shock its readers long after they have heard it interpreted as a celebration of God's freedom to grace the last and the least in whatever way he chooses. However promising the explanations, however ingeniously they are served up by preachers and scholars, many people feel unwilling to relinquish the questions that continue to bother them. There remains for many the residual suspicion that the first-hired workers have somehow been cheated.

Is it fair that a group of labourers who labour throughout a twelve-hour working day are paid the same as those who have worked for one hour? Although the first-hired are paid the sum originally promised by the landowner, are they right to be upset not only about the final payment and how it is done but because they feel that their labour has been diminished by the selective generosity of the vineyard owner? If employers "value" their workforce by paying them appropriate wages, what value is put on those who have laboured most when they are paid the same as those who have laboured least? How could the vineyard owner run his business *another day* on the same principles? In the same vein, it may be instructive for the psalmist to warn, "In vain you get up earlier, and put off going to bed, sweating to make a living, since he provides for his beloved as they sleep" (Ps 127:2, JB); indeed, but the psalmist would hardly expect his listeners to give up sweating and opt for dozing as a lifestyle blessed by God.

As J.R. Donahue notes: "Hardly any parable in the Gospels seems to upset the basic structure of an orderly society as does this one."[1] The parable seems to turn conventional wisdom on its head and overturn the ordinary values that most people unthinkingly subscribe to:

> *In life you are rewarded according to your efforts;*
> *in work you are paid according to your time and labour;*
> *the measure that you put into life is the measure that you will receive back.*

The parable seems to introduce a contrary wisdom without warning: some people are rewarded not according to their efforts but because of the selective choice of their patrons. Sometimes in life we are lucky and we receive what we did not expect or deserve; sometimes we are enriched because of the favour and kindness of others. More importantly, we believe that we are constantly enriched by the mercy of God, and that it would be folly to stand before God and ask him to treat us according to our deserts. We believe with Shakespeare:

> Though justice be thy plea, consider this –
> That in the course of justice none of us
> Should see salvation; we do pray for mercy,

And that same prayer doth teach us all to render
The deeds of mercy.
                    (*The Merchant of Venice*, Act IV, Scene iii)

While all this is true, *is it the point of this parable?* Commentators have traditionally agreed with the landowner in his right to do what he pleases with his money. Even if we reluctantly agree with this, an underlying question still presses: why does the landowner organise the payment in such a way that it is calculated to upset the first-hired labourers? Is his decision to reward the latecomers first and fully an act of charity or a calculated insult disguised as kindness? Is this a parable about the freedom of God to grace whomsoever he pleases, to demonstrate that his ways are not our ways? Or is it a story that encodes the absolute authority of rich landowners to lord it over day labourers and make their authority felt by choosing to treat these expendables however they please?

The context
The parable appears only in Matthew's Gospel, and the evangelist inserts it into a section where he has been following Mark's structure closely. Before the parable Matthew 19:1-30 parallels Mark 10:1-31; after the parable Matthew 20:17-34 rejoins his source, paralleling Mark 10:32-52. Matthew's decision to place the parable in this context has exerted a clear influence on how it is usually interpreted.

> Departure from Galilee and arrival in Judea 19:1-2
> Dispute with the Pharisees on divorce 19:3-9
> Clarification to the disciples 19:10-12
> The blessing of the children 19:13-15
> The rich young man turns away from Jesus' call 19:16-22
> Jesus teaches his disciples about the danger of riches 19:23-26
> The disciples' place in the kingdom is affirmed 19:27-30
> *"But many that are first will be last, and the last first."* 19:30
> **The Parable of the Labourers in the Vineyard** *20:1-15*
> *"So the last will be first, and the first last."* 20:16

What began as a dispute with the Pharisees ends with the assurance of the unique place of Jesus' own disciples: that reversal is summarised in the narrative with the axiom: "Many that are first will be last, and the last first." Commenting on Matthew's interpretation B.B. Scott writes: "The first who will be last are the Pharisees, those who have tested the Lord and failed (in the divorce question), and those last who will be first are the disciples, who are promised to sit on thrones of Israel. The parable of the labourers in the vineyard confirms this position. The latecomers are the disciples, and those first hired are the Pharisees. Furthermore, the lord of the parable is Jesus as judge – a frequent theme in Matthew's parables."[2] There seems little doubt that Matthew is using the parable to advance his theme that the first shall be last, and his addition of verse 16 to the parable ("So the last will be first, and the first last") confirms his intention – particularly when the verse lies uneasily with the action of the parable where the issue is not one of reversal but equality of reward.

Matthew's placement of the parable has effectively governed its interpretation. The majority of commentators would see the owner of the vineyard as a figure of God, those hired first as the Pharisees or the Jewish people, and those hired last as the disciples or the Gentiles. There has been little variation from C.H. Dodd's interpretation, originally published in 1935: "The point of the story is that the employer, out of sheer generosity and compassion for the unemployed, pays as large a wage to those who have worked for one hour as to those who have worked all day. It is a striking picture of the divine generosity which gives without regard to the measures of strict justice."[3] In focusing on the graciousness and beneficence of the owner of the vineyard, most commentators agree with the landowner's interpretation of his own behaviour when he claims not only that he is doing no wrong but that he is being provocatively generous.

To free the parables from an evangelist's editorial framework is not, as B. Gerhardsson dramatically contests, to "treat them as wild texts designed to function as naked narratives with indeterminable messages".[4] Rather it is, in this case, to look at the story in its own right – a dispute between day labourers and a rich landowner – and be open to the possibility that we might arrive at different conclusions from those previously recorded. There are two voices appealing to the reader: the voice of the first-hired who say that their work has been diminished by the landowner's decision to reward the last-hired the same as them; the voice of the landowner justifying his choice as generous. Which voice do we believe more accurately reflects what is happening in the payment?

Landowners and landless day labourers

Jesus' original audience would have had to make no imaginative leap to understand the principal figures in the parable, the landowner and landless day labourers, who were familiar social types in the agrarian society of first-century Palestine as they were throughout the Roman empire. The Roman senator Marcus Tullius Cicero (executed 43 BC) wrote to his son Marcus, a student in Athens, advising him about traditional moral judgements regarding various occupations:

> Now in regard to trades and other means of livelihood, which ones are to be considered becoming to a gentleman and which ones are vulgar, we have been taught, in general, as follows. First those means of livelihood are rejected as undesirable which incur people's ill-will, as those of tax-gatherers and usurers. Unbecoming to a gentleman, too, and vulgar are the means of livelihood of all hired workmen whom we pay for mere manual labour, not for artistic skill; for in their case the very wages they receive is a pledge of their slavery . . . But of all the occupations by which gain is secured, none is better than agriculture, none more profitable, none more delightful, none more becoming to a freeman.[5]

When Cicero speaks about agriculture as the most profitable means of livelihood for a gentleman, he is referring to agriculture conducted by the landed gentry on their estates, not to the manual work of the day labourer. In an agrarian society the summit of respectability is seen in membership of the land-owning elite, whose independence and style of life are financed by the "vulgar" manual workers. The elite manage the land, in the sense of determining which crops will be the most profitable to grow; they do not work the land themselves, any more than the owner of the vineyard in the parable works in his vineyard. In verse 8 of the parable, the landowner is called *ho kurios tou ampelōnos*, literally, "lord of the vineyard".

Commenting on the social world of Galilee as it appears in the Gospels, S. Freyne writes: "At one end of the scale there are large landowners who have hired servants or a steward, and at the other end we meet day-labourers, slaves, and the destitute who do not participate at all – the beggars, the blind, the maimed and the lame. In between are the small landowners or share-croppers, living in one-roomed houses with their families."[6] In the parable the lord of the vineyard enjoys the privileged life at the top of the scale – he has a steward or manager (verse 8, *epitropos*) whose presence implies that his master belongs to the governing classes that employed stewards. As we saw in the previous chapter, stewards or retainers were employed to ensure their master's riches continued to grow, to manage his business in his absence, and to oversee his servants or any casual labourers who were employed.

As G. Lenski and many others have pointed out, there was no middle class in agrarian societies as in modern industrial societies: there was the land-owning governing class and there was the rest of the population, in various degrees of dependency on their masters. Even the retainers, who acted as a buffer group between the governing class and the lower classes, were wholly dependent on the patron-client relationship they temporarily enjoyed. They could be dismissed if they brought displeasure to their master, and that expulsion would, in all probability, catapult them to the bottom of the social heap. Thus the dismissed steward in Luke's parable of The Dishonest Steward contemplates life as an *expendable* on hearing news of his dismissal from the great household: "What shall I do, since my master is taking the stewardship away from me? I am not strong enough to dig, and I am ashamed to beg" (Lk 16:3). The only options open to him after dismissal are working as a day labourer or begging on the streets.

The division between the governing, land-owning class and all those below them is difficult to imagine in our industrial society today. On this point G. Lenski notes: "One fact impresses itself on almost every observer of agrarian societies, especially on one who views them in a broadly comparative perspective. This is the fact of *marked social inequality*. Without exception, one finds pronounced differences in power, privilege, and honour associated with mature agrarian economies. These differences surpass those found even in the most stratified horticultural societies of Africa and the New World, and far exceed those found in simple horticultural or hunting and gathering societies."[7]

That social inequality is demonstrably clear in the divide between the land-owning elite and day labourers. In Lenski's social stratification, shown in the previous chapter, day labourers belonged to the lowest group in society, the *expendables*: they existed because "despite high rates of infant mortality, the occasional practice of infanticide, the more frequent practice of celibacy, and adult mortality caused by war, famine, and disease, agrarian societies usually produced *more people than the dominant classes found it profitable to employ*".[8]

Most peasant farmers could not afford to divide their small patrimony among all their children: excess children were eventually sent to the market places in the hope they would be hired as day labourers at planting or harvest time. Peasants who lost their only security of land to the owners of large estates also moved down the scale into this group and were forced to become itinerant day labourers. As L. Schottroff observes: "As estates became larger, the number of day labourers would grow."[9] In an agricultural world, this surplus labour force was needed only at times of planting and harvest. With a market of labour that was far in excess of what was required, and with no social security other than the family, many of these expendables were forced to beg on the streets of the major towns and cities; many became social bandits who survived from stealing until they were hunted down and then sold as slaves or executed as common criminals.

Obviously in times of hardship and famine, the ranks of the expendables would be considerably expanded. As W.R. Herzog notes: "For the expendables, life was brutal and brief; characteristically, they lasted no more than five to seven years after entering this class, but the size of the expendable class remained more or less stable because its ranks were being constantly replenished from the classes of peasants, artisans, merchants, and the unclean and degraded immediately above it."[10] Downward mobility was clearly a constant threat to the vast majority of the population, peasants who lived in a society which had no sure protection beyond the uncommon advantage of belonging to a family that could afford to absorb their loss. When anyone ended up in the expendable class, the first rude awakening was probably the realisation that they had no bargaining power, that they relied totally on patronage and others' rare need of them. This lack of bargaining power is reflected at the heart of the parable.

The structure of the parable

Scene 1: The Hiring
a) A householder goes out early in the morning, to hire day labourers to work in his vineyard. After agreeing with them for a denarius a day, he sends them off to work.
b) The owner goes out again at 9 am, midday and 3 pm, and commands the labourers to work in his vineyard, promising to pay them whatever is right.
c) The owner returns to the market place about 5 pm and questions the unemployed about why they are still idle. They reply that no one has hired them. The owner commands them to go to his vineyard. There is no mention of payment.

Scene 2: The Payment
a) At 6 pm the landowner instructs his steward to pay the wages, beginning with those hired last. They are paid one denarius.
b) Those hired first expect more, but they are also paid one denarius. They complain to the landowner that those hired last, who have not borne the burden or the heat of the day, have been treated the same as them.
c) Addressing one of them, the landowner justifies what he has done and points to the original agreement. He justifies his freedom in choosing to do what he likes with his own money and questions their envy at his generosity.

The hiring of the day labourers

The drama begins early in the morning, at sunrise. While we know the time of the day – around six o'clock in the morning – we are not told the time of the year. In all probability it is harvest time, when the vintage and the pressing have to be completed before the rains come. A heavy yield of grapes or a late harvest would explain why the owner of the vineyard is so anxious to hire additional workers to supplement his labour force, not only throughout the day but even an hour before sunset.

The five trips the owner makes to the market place, to hire workers, are an indication not only of the urgency of the work but of the size of the vineyard. Such a large property, with such a luxury harvest as grapes, points to an owner whose social standing is that of a gentleman farmer – the kind of occupation that

Cicero recommends so ardently to his son. No peasant farmer could afford either to retain the office of a steward or to hire day labourers. While B.B. Scott is undoubtedly right in his observation that in Israel's stock of imagery "Vineyards have a strong metaphorical potential",[11] perhaps what is more to the point in this parable is that vineyards also have a strong economic potential. As W.R. Herzog notes: "Vineyards were most likely owned by elites because they produce a crop that can be converted into a luxury item (wine), monetized, and exported. A vineyard also represents a major capital investment during the initial four years of its existence when it is not bearing fruit but requires constant tending."[12] In Lenski's social stratification of classes in agrarian societies (see Figure 1 in previous chapter) the vineyard owner would belong to the land-owning governing classes.

What remains puzzling is that the owner of the vineyard does not use his steward, who appears later in the story, to manage the hiring as he does the payment. A rich landowner would normally be protected from direct contact with manual labourers through the agency of his steward, yet this parable brings the owner to the foreground, making him visible both at the hiring and at the payment. Through this dramatic device the original listener and the reader see representatives of two social groups that would normally never meet, a member of the governing class and members of the expendables. Depending on your interpretation of the parable, the deliberate visibility of the vineyard owner serves to focus on him as a man of remarkable kindness or it reveals the hidden face of power by showing us a man who protects his investments by hiring expendables on his own terms and paying them whatever he pleases.

Only with the first-hired does the owner agree on a denarius for a day's labour. Most commentators who argue for a denarius as a normal or fare wage for a day's labour use this parable as proof of their point, nearly always within the larger understanding that the owner is a God figure and a man of unusual kindness. Certainly there was no established minimum wage: while employers were free to bargain on any terms they could get the unemployed to accept, the unemployed were hardly in a position to negotiate the terms of their employment. The unemployed had to accept what was offered or walk away: in a world where the labour market far exceeded the labour required, few unemployed people could afford to walk away. It was for this reason that, as M. Katz points out, the later rabbinic writing on employment ethics focused wholly on the rights of workers.[13]

It is very difficult to know if the denarius was a just daily wage for labourers or to discover its equivalent value today. B.B. Scott concludes his comments on the denarius thus: "Because of lack of hard evidence, inflation, and the variation in local conditions, a precise value for a denarius cannot be determined. The evidence suggests that a wage of a denarius a day would be sufficient to support a worker and his family at *subsistence* level, that is, at the level of a peasant. In no way can it be viewed as a wage generating a surplus. Of itself the wage is not generous."[14] Given that the expendables *might* find employment in the rural areas at times of planting and harvest – even in the parable there are unemployed labourers still looking for work one hour before sunset – the money they fitfully managed to earn would have had to support them for much longer than a day. In that calculation, apart from the fact that there was no work available on the sabbath, one can only wonder if a denarius for a day's labour was sufficient to live on. Whatever it was, it was certainly not a generous reward for labouring twelve hours in the day.

The owner returns to the market place (*agora*), the regular assembly place for the unemployed, to hire workers at various "hours" throughout the day. The working day, which began at sunrise and ended with sunset, was divided into twelve hours: thus the third hour is 9 am, the sixth hour is midday, the ninth hour is 3 pm, and the eleventh hour is 5 pm. When he returns on his second visit to the market place the owner sees others standing idle; he commands them to go to the vineyard and, without naming any specific wage, tells them "whatever is right I will give you". Without protest, the unemployed do as he says. The absence of any wage agreement is an indication not only of the owner's unilateral power to determine what is right but also of the workers' lack of bargaining power. With a surfeit of labour flooding the market – which has the inevitable consequence of depressed wages – the unemployed have no say in determining the worth of their own labour; they have to take the risk that their employers might pay them trifling sums for their toil.

That arrangement between the vineyard owner and day labourers, where the owner promises payment but leaves the sum unspoken, is repeated at midday and around three in the afternoon. When the owner makes his final trip to the market place at 5 pm, the transaction is different. He first questions those who are there, "Why do you stand here idle all day?" The question seems rather strange since the owner, even at this late hour, is urgently looking for workers. Rather than being relieved he has found a number of them, his question indicates disapproval that these expendables are still not profitably employed.

The labourers explain, without comment or complaint, that they are idle because no one has hired them. There seems to be no warrant to posit, as J. Jeremias does, that their excuse "is an idle evasion . . . a cover for their typical oriental indifference".[15] Their response does, however, provoke the question: if these workers have been waiting for employment in the market place all day, why did the owner not hire them earlier in the day? That question remains unanswered. He orders them to go to the vineyard, but this time he says nothing about wages, speaks no promise about paying whatever he deems right. His command concludes the scene; it is taken for granted that the unemployed in their desperate need will obey him.

The payment

At the end of the day's labour in the vineyard, the time comes for payment, as the Law demanded: "You shall not withhold the wages of poor and needy labourers, whether other Israelites or aliens who reside in your land in one of your towns. You shall pay them their wages daily before sunset, because they are poor and their livelihood depends on them; otherwise they might cry to the Lord against you, and you would incur guilt" (Dt 24:14-15). In this parable the cry the early labourers will make is not to the Lord but to the lord of the vineyard.

Before payment is made, the lord (*kyrios*) of the vineyard intervenes to tell his steward to pay the labourers, beginning with the last and ending with the first-hired. At this point the order of payment is revealed to the reader but not the payment. The lord deliberately arranges the reversal of normal procedure, so that the first-hired will build up their hopes when they see what the later workers are paid. If the owner of the vineyard wanted only to be "charitable" to the workers he employed at later stages in the day, it would have been sufficient to leave his steward to pay each group in the order they were hired, with the only instruction to pay all the workers the same. That customary method of payment, even with the uncustomary calculation of payment, would have upset no one – except, possibly, the reader.

The parable confines its interest to one group of workers, telling us that the early workers receive the same wage as the last-hired. By now there is such a large cast of characters, hired at five different times during the day, that it would clearly lessen the dramatic effect of the parable to go through them, group by group. The presumption is that all the workers receive a denarius, although the text does not state this. Nor does the text tell us how any of the other workers respond to the landowner's decision to pay everyone the same: we are not told, for instance, if their response matches the landowner's estimation of himself – that he is a generous and just man. The interest is focused on the dissatisfied workers. Even though D. Via regards the early workers as grumblers, he points to their importance in the structure of the parable: "this parable is the story of the grumbling full-day workers; and exegesis has usually not been sufficiently attentive to this fact. These workers are allowed a recognition scene, and it is their changing fortune which gives the parable its formal shape."[16]

The first workers have to wait for their payment until the end, observing in the meantime the amount the others receive. As they see what the others are paid their expectation grows that they will be paid more; their natural expectation, however, primes them for disappointment. *They make no objection about the amount the others are paid*, but when they receive the same as the others they register their complaint, comparing the last-hired who have worked only an hour with themselves – who have borne the burden of a full day's labour and endured the burning heat. They believe it is unfair to reward such manifestly unequal labour with equal wages, to devalue their twelve-hour labour by publicly according it the same value as one hour's work in the cool of the evening.

However one interprets the parable, it is natural to have a measure of sympathy with the early workers. It is difficult not to see what they clearly suspect: that in deliberately organising the method of payment and the wages in the way he does, the landowner succeeds both in publicly shaming them and in devaluing their labour.

The owner picks out the spokesman of the group and addresses him as "Friend". The idea that this dissatisfied expendable – who has the temerity to object to how a rich landowner treats his workers – is suddenly elevated to being a friend of the elite is obviously ironic. Paradoxically, the landowner's use of the term "friend" to a labourer reinforces the marked social difference between the two men. Anxious to justify himself, the owner goes on to argue that he is doing the leader of the early workers no wrong: "Did you not *agree with me* for one denarius?" The owner may be deceiving himself and his listeners if he interprets the earlier transaction between himself as a powerful landowner and an underclass that suffers from chronic deprivation as a free *agreement*, as if the expendables were in a position to bargain and come to a mutually acceptable arrangement between themselves and the landowner. It comes as no surprise that in the matter of payment, as the landowner admits, it is the labourers who agreed with him, not vice versa. The deprived can take it or leave it; if they take it, are they agreeing or simply submitting to a decision made unilaterally by a powerful landowner?

The scene appears to end with the landowner's command that the worker takes what belongs to him and goes, a dismissal that sounds as if it has the touch of the eternal about it. But the landowner is still anxious to justify himself, and he goes on to underline his freedom of choice: "I choose to give (*dounai*) to this last as I give to you." Is this an insight into the landowner's peculiar belief in his own goodness and generosity: that as the payment to the last workers was his gift, so even the payment to the early workers is his gift? If this is so, he fails to recognise the simple truth that the early workers have *earned* their money; their wages, whatever else they might be, are not the landowner's gift.

The landowner is clearly insistent in defending his honour as he continues to question those who do not see things the way he does. The more he defends himself, the more he reveals himself. He now asks: "Am I not allowed to do what I choose with what belongs to me? Or do you begrudge my generosity?" Earlier the rich landowner promised to do "*whatever is right*"; now he admits, more truthfully, if more desperately, that he is free to do *whatever he likes* with his own resources. He is no longer appealing to customary practice or to justice, but to his own freedom to treat people as he pleases with his own resources. How did this rich landowner come by his resources, anyway, particularly his entitlement to the land?

In the tradition of Israel it is God who owns the landowner's land; the landowner himself is God's tenant. As W. Janzen points out, the frequent listing of the *former* owners of the land in the Hebrew Bible – land that is now inhabited by Israel – is a frequent reminder that the newcomers do not own it, since it was given to them by God.[17] The land laws of Leviticus 25 deliberately set out to protect the small man from permanently losing the little land he has to rich landowners. As W. Eichrodt comments: "Here the law of redemption sets bounds *which refuse any one person unrestricted rights over his landed property*. . . In these circumstances any outright sale of land was excluded, any such sale being in effect until the next year of Jubilee. What has really happened is that the sale of lease is substituted for freehold tenure. There is no means of telling whether this law was ever enforced or whether it remained simply an ideal requirement."[18] One thing is clear: in announcing the absolute right over what he owns the lord of the vineyard is putting himself in the place of the Lord of the land.

The landowner's final question (literally translated: "Is your eye evil because I am good?") again professes his own goodness, at the same time openly entertaining the idea that the early workers, in protesting against his judgement, are envious at his goodness. It does not seem to strike him that they might be protesting against his *meanness to them*, not his payment to the others, that they might be angry at how his "generosity" exhausted itself before it reached them. The workers have not suggested that because they have been paid a denarius, the owner should have paid the last-hired only one-twelfth of a denarius – which would be a paltry sum; they were asking that his benevolence, which has touched *every other group he has hired* in the course of the day, should also profit them.

I think it is worth noting that if we take the last-hired workers out of the calculation, the promise the landowner made to the workers hired between 9 am and 3 pm was that he would pay them "whatever is right" – a calculation he would presumably make according to customary practice and his own judgement. If at the end of the day *these* workers are paid a denarius, how can a denarius for a twelve-hour day – according to the landowner's professed standards – now be considered *right*? More importantly, is he the only person in the parable who has a say in defining what is just and right?

Perception of what is just or right is at the heart of the matter, and it is the landowner who insistently defines what is right in the parable: he has the uncontested power to decide who deserves what, who should benefit from his "generous" manner and who should not. R. Ford argues that the wealthy landowner is using his apparent generosity to cover up his control:

> If one does not notice his prior position of total control over the essential definitions, the landowner indeed appears to be generous. (Traditional readings rely on his generosity to render him a figure of God.) Yet oppressed people the world over are endlessly familiar with the differences between what is held out to them as lawful and what they themselves perceive to be just . . . Our identification with the wealthy tempts us not to question the owner's point of view. Listeners who are poor may know better;

they may recognise that the rich have the last word not because they have a firmer grasp on reality but simply because that is how it is with wealthy people.[19]

When you look at the two speeches in this confrontation scene, you notice that the landowner's speech is over twice as long as that of the early workers. One wonders, in the end, if the landowner protests too much; one wonders if his anxiety to prove that he is not only generous but also just in his dealings with his day labourers is indeed well founded.

Reflection

In the course of this analysis we have tried to look at the parable in its own right, rather than interpret it within the editorial frame provided by Matthew. It is a story of confrontation between a rich landowner who believes he is both just and generous in the way he treats his day labourers and a group of those labourers who feel aggrieved at the way they have been treated by him. Two opposing voices speak to us, two voices that are clearly competing for our understanding and support – the voice of the early workers and the voice of the landowner. We can support only one reading of reality, the landowner's or the workers' version. Only those outside the parable, the listeners, can come to a judgement on the matter, and that judgement is certainly not an easy one to make. Perhaps more than any other parable in the Gospels, the parable of The Labourers in the Vineyard tells us that our work as listeners begins when the parable ends: we have to work out its meaning.

If we believe that the lord of the vineyard is a God figure, inevitably we have to interpret his actions as generous and the complaint of the early workers against him as unjustified. We will argue that his generosity expresses his gracious freedom to benefit the latecomers in life, and that what he does is not an act of spiteful arbitrariness. We will maintain that he is indeed good, as he claims, because he graces the destitute expendables with an equal share in his property rather than simply rewarding them according to merit. With this lord, everyone is equally graced; if we cannot understand that, as the early workers cannot, we have missed his subversive teaching.

If, however, we believe that the lord of the vineyard is a representative type of the landowning elite in Palestine, we are at least free to look at how he behaves and to question his declared motives. We might, of course, reach the same conclusions as those who believe him to be a God figure, but this will not be because we are simply genuflecting to his omnipotent presence and his authoritative reading of reality.

If we believe that Jesus, not Matthew, is encoding in this parable the common practice of a landowning elite who have the freedom and the power to treat their workers how they please, we will interpret the parable differently from the traditional way. We might notice that the way the lord of the vineyard pays the wages succeeds in dividing the workforce, so that the group of day labourers who share the same fate as expendables lose whatever solidarity they shared. In paying workers who have worked different hours the same amount, we will argue that the owner creates division by apparent equality.

If we read the parable in this way we will see the early workers as heroes rather than villains, because they articulate, however awkwardly, the ancient hurt of being exploited. And then, when they make their protest, we will notice how they are blamed by their rich master as the architects of their own misery. Thus, we will argue, the victims of injustice are reproached for the unjust situation they find themselves in, one that has been deftly organised by their powerful employer.

Does this parable reveal what the kingdom of God is like or does it disclose what the kingdom of God is not? Only the reader can decide.

[1] J.R. Donahue, *The Gospel in Parables* (Philadelphia: Fortress Press, 1988) p.81

[2] B.B. Scott, *Hear Then the Parable* (Minneapolis: Fortress, 1989) p.285

[3] C.H. Dodd, *The Parables of the Kingdom* (London: Collins, 1967) p.92

[4] B. Gerhardsson, "If We Do Not Cut the Parables out of Their Frames" in *New Testament Studies* 37 (1991) p.335

[5] Cicero, *De Officiis* 1.150-151, quoted in J.D. Crossan, *The Historical Jesus: the Life of a Mediterranean Jewish Peasant* (Edinburgh: T&T Clark, 1993) pp.52-53

[6] S. Freyne, *Galilee, Jesus and the Gospels* (Dublin: Gill & Macmillan, 1988) p.95

[7] G.E. Lenski, *Power and Privilege,* p.210

[8] G.E. Lenski, *Power and Privilege,* pp.281-282

[9] L. Schottroff & W. Stegemann, *Jesus and the Hope of the Poor* (New York: Orbis, 1986) p.133

[10] W.R. Herzog, *Parables as Subversive Speech,* p.66

[11] B.B. Scott, *Hear Then the Parable,* p.290

[12] W.R. Herzog, *Parables as Subversive Speech,* p.85

[13] M. Katz, *Protection of the Weak in the Talmud* (New York: Columbia University Press, 1935) p.30

[14] B.B. Scott, *Hear Then the Parable,* p.291

[15] J. Jeremias, *The Parables of Jesus,* p.37

[16] D. Via, *The Parables* (Philadelphia: Fortress, 1967) p.150

[17] W. Janzen, "Land" in *The Anchor Bible Dictionary* Vol 4 p.144

[18] W. Eichrodt, *Theology of the Old Testament* Vol 1 (London: SCM, 1969) pp.96, 97

[19] R. Ford, *The Parables of Jesus,* pp.118, 121

Matthew 18:23-35 (NRSV)

[23]*"For this reason the kingdom of heaven may be compared to a king who wished to settle accounts with his slaves.* [24]*When he began the reckoning, one who owed him ten thousand talents was brought to him;* [25]*and, as he could not pay, his lord ordered him to be sold, together with his wife and children and all his possessions, and payment to be made.* [26]*So the slave fell on his knees before him, saying, 'Have patience with me, and I will pay you everything.'* [27]*And out of pity for him, the lord of that slave released him and forgave him the debt.*

[28]*"But that same slave, as he went out, came upon one of his fellow slaves who owed him a hundred denarii; and seizing him by the throat, he said, 'Pay what you owe.'* [29]*Then his fellow slave fell down and pleaded with him, 'Have patience with me, and I will pay you.'* [30]*But he refused; then he went and threw him into prison until he would pay the debt.*

[31]*"When his fellow slaves saw what had happened, they were greatly distressed, and they went and reported to their lord all that had taken place.* [32]*Then his lord summoned him and said to him, 'You wicked slave! I forgave you all that debt because you pleaded with me.* [33]*Should you not have had mercy on your fellow slave, as I had mercy on you?'* [34]*And in anger his lord handed him over to be tortured until he would pay his entire debt.* [35]*So my heavenly Father will also do to every one of you, if you do not forgive your brother or sister from your heart."*

The context of Matthew 18

Chapter 18 of Matthew's Gospel is a remarkable piece of writing: in the fourth of the five great discourses of this Gospel, Matthew gathers sayings from diverse origins and assembles them together in an address given by Jesus to his disciples. The sayings deal with issues and problems that arise in the life of an organised Christian community, making the whole discourse a reflection on church life and order. In this community Jesus is present, not in the flesh, but in the spirit, wherever two or three are gathered in his name (18:20). Directed at those who have pastoral responsibility in the church and exercise authority, the discourse is conspicuous for its total lack of hierarchical figures. In Matthew it is the community of the faithful who are the ultimate court of appeal.

The discourse is divided into two main sections, each ending with a parable:

1st part: Care for children and the little ones (18:1-14)
2nd part: Care for the sinful brother or sister (18:15-35)

The whole discourse focuses on relationships within the Christian community, on the conditions necessary for a healthy interaction among the followers of Jesus. The problems of living together as a community are explored: the church must always have a secure place for the little people in the community; the church must come to terms with scandal, members who get lost, sinful members who find it hard to welcome correction, and the tendency of the righteous in the community to set limits on forgiveness. Summarising the discourse, J.P. Meier comments: "In other words, the basic problem in church life is sin, and the basic solution is the mercy of the Father."[1]

The chapter opens with the disciples' question: "Who is the greatest in the kingdom of heaven?" The imagery of kingdom naturally raises issues of prestige and power, issues that Jesus earlier regarded as a temptation of the devil (Mt 4:5-10). Matthew is going to argue that the norms of greatness that function in society cannot be the norms that function in the kingdom, where Jesus' standards must prevail: thus Matthew deprecates any insistence on rank and dignity in the Christian fellowship. The illustration of Jesus' contrary wisdom is made when he takes a child and puts the child among the disciples; he then challenges his disciples to change their thinking about importance in the community: "Whoever welcomes one such child in my name welcomes me." In Jesus' eyes, the absence of power, not power, is what makes a person great in the kingdom.

The next section (verses 6-9) retains the child as a symbol of simple and unpretentious discipleship, and Jesus warns his disciples against scandalising "one of these little ones". Again special sensitivity is required by leaders towards those who are the most vulnerable in the community. Immediately following (verses 10-14) is a warning never to despise the little people in the community, including a parable where pastoral responsibility for the lost is given primacy of place.

Dealing with the straying one is also the theme of the following section (verses 15-18). If another member of the church sins against you, you must go and point out the fault when the two of you are alone. In this injunction there is the challenge for *everyone* in the community to exercise his or her own leadership in resolving disputes and in the act of forgiving. The scenario begins in confrontation between the one who has offended and the person offended: the first step is for the offended one to seek reconciliation privately. This is rarely what happens in church life. If

110

a parishioner is offended by another parishioner, usually he or she goes to the parish priest. If parishioners are offended by what the parish priest is doing, they usually go to the bishop. If they are offended by what the bishop is doing, they go to the cardinal. If they do not like what the cardinal is doing, they appeal to Rome. Usually the last thing people do is actually *confront the one who is offending them.*

For Matthew, confrontation is an essential part of forgiveness. Instead of doing this, however, people usually appeal to hierarchy, and the problem of appealing to hierarchy will be illustrated in the parable when the fellow slaves do not confront the offending slave but appeal to the king. The difficulty with that, of course, is that it leaves no higher court of appeal.

If personal confrontation fails, the offended person is not to bring it to the attention of the whole community, but to attempt to straighten things out by getting the help of one or two others. The ultimate court of appeal is the community itself, who have the power to expel recalcitrant members. That said, however, the question begs: if the shunned member is to be treated like a tax collector, how did Jesus treat tax collectors? The community is not finished with those whom it expels, an interpretation that is reinforced by the following section (verses 21-22) where Jesus reminds Peter that the obligation to forgive is without end. As R.E. Brown comments:

> Evidently Matthew had lived long enough with that authority to know its dangers. Experience teaches that organised societies are more likely to abuse authority than to abdicate it. The order in chapt. 18 proclaims that the power to forgive indefinitely is a greater Christian possession than the power to excommunicate. Lest it be accused of laxness, the church is often very careful about forgiving. Yet, the number of people who have turned away from the church because they found it too forgiving is infinitesimal; the number who have turned away because they found it unforgiving is legion. For this reason, Matthew's pastoral judgement on those in the church who refuse forgiveness is the very harsh conclusion of the parable. In their case the Matthean Jesus has defined the unforgivable sin: it is to be unforgiving.[2]

The immediate context of the parable is Peter's question: how much should we forgive? The answer of Jesus is that there is no arithmetical end to forgiveness, for it is the endless duty of his followers to offer clemency. The parable sits uneasily within that context for it contains no example of *repeated* forgiveness. While the parable is not a good illustration of Jesus' answer to Peter, Matthew's addition in verse 35 clearly establishes the evangelist's concern to draw the parable into the wider context of the forgiveness in the community. In so doing Matthew transposes the story into allegory, identifying the king with God: "So my heavenly Father will also do to every one of you, if you do not forgive your brother or sister from your heart" (Mt 18:35). Along with the majority of commentators, our reading of the parable will attribute the introductory "kingdom of heaven" formula (verse 23a) and the concluding moral (verse 35) to Matthew's editorial hand.

Kings and slave-retainers

The king is the male sovereign ruler, who acts as a central symbol for the territory and population he rules over, as well as personifying its prosperity and security. Monarchy has been the most popular form of government in agrarian societies throughout history, and the king was responsible for the maintenance of law and order through the use of military force and a centralised bureaucracy. In agrarian societies the king and the whole of the elite classes were dependent on the extraction of an agricultural surplus from the peasants in order to provide for their subsistence needs. The king had the power to command various forms of taxation, and his central bureaucracy provided the means whereby he was able to control the various levels of government responsible for the military, economic, legal and ritual activities of the network of cities and villages within the state.

The king was the legal owner of the institutions of the state. As K. Whitelam comments: "Probably the most important aspect of kingship therefore in an agrarian society was the ownership of agricultural land. The development of a monarchy means in reality the transfer of sovereignty over agricultural land from the villages to the king. In practice, arable land was granted to various royal functionaries as hereditary estates, securing patrimonial land tenure in return for taxes and military service . . . Elite landlords extracted from their peasant cultivators as much as 50 per cent or more of all produce in the form of taxation and rent. They in turn paid taxes, rent and labour to the king."[3] This system of land tenure and taxation maintained the distribution of power and privilege in the stratified world of agrarian societies.

The ruler had a vested interest in maintaining a ruling elite who were loyal to him while at the same time preventing them from becoming too powerful; he could manage to keep the ruling class divided through promoting the causes of those he favoured temporarily. Because endemic feuding and honest graft fed the entire system, the ruler would often change his heads of department to keep corruption and ambition within manageable grounds. In a patron/client world the competition was intense for the favour of the ultimate patron, the king, a fact that could be used well by an enterprising monarch. The conflict over wealth, status and power never ceased; everything was for sale, including justice, favours, office, and influence; nothing could be taken for granted; everything was dependent on the selective favour of the reigning king or on his chosen advisers.

T. Carney describes antiquity as "a society based on patronage, not class stratification; so little pyramids of power abounded . . . Thus society resembles a mass of little pyramids of influence, each headed by a major family – or one giant pyramid headed by an autocrat – not the three-decker sandwich of upper, middle, and lower classes familiar to us from industrial society."[4] Thus when the king withdraws his patronage at the conclusion of the parable, the withdrawal is absolute. There can be no further appeal.

The king and the governing class needed a bureaucracy to put their policies into practice; this gave rise to the retainer class who were dedicated to implementing the policies of the ruler and the landowning elite. T. Carney divides the retainers into three groups, beginning with the lowest: "the *illiterati* (porters, gaolers, etc.), the *litterati* (scribes, lawyers, accountants) and possessors of *dignitates* (high official positions)".[5] The slaves (*douloi*) in the parable are highly positioned dignitaries in the service of the king. Their designation as slaves indicates their total dependence on the ruler and on his patronage but, as we noted in chapter four, slaves could hold positions of high importance in the court of the ruler.

The unmerciful slave is a highly positioned retainer who has won the trust of the king: as an individual close to the king he is in a position to use his privileged access to amass his own fortune through patronage. He is probably the equivalent of a Chancellor of the Exchequer, a high official who oversees the financial government of the kingdom, someone who decides what tribute and other form of taxes should be collected. He is responsible for managing the transfer of the economic surplus of the people of the realm to his king and chief patron. In the process of so doing, he has failed to deliver to the king the proper amount. This provides the opening conflict of the parable.

The structure of the parable

Reckoning 1

a) King confronts slave who owes him 10,000 talents (60m denarii).

b) The slave cannot pay. The king passes judgement: the slave, his family and all his possessions are to be sold, to meet the debt.

c) The slave falls on his knees at the king's feet, pleading: "Have patience with me, and I will pay you everything."

d) Out of pity, the king releases the slave and cancels the debt.

Reckoning 2

a) As he leaves, the slave meets a fellow slave who owes him 100 denarii.

b) He seizes him by the throat and and says: "Pay what you owe."

c) Second slave falls down at his fellow slave's feet, pleading: "Have patience with me and I will pay you."

d) First slave refuses, and throws his fellow slave into prison until he can pay the debt.

Reckoning 3

a) When his fellow slaves see this they are greatly distressed.

b) They go to the king and report the whole affair.

c) The king summons the first slave and says: "You wicked slave! I forgave you all that debt because you pleaded with me. Should you not have had mercy on your fellow slave, as I had mercy on you?"

d) In his anger the king hands over first slave to the torturers until the debt is paid.

The first reckoning

The first scene opens with a king checking his income from the taxes collected by his high officials. When he begins the reckoning one of the king's slaves who owes him ten thousand talents is brought before him. The talent was the largest

114

currency unit in the entire Near East – worth about 6,000 denarii – and ten thousand was also the largest number used in counting. Ten thousand talents is an unimaginable sum of money – Josephus says that the sum of Herod's annual taxation of Judea amounted to 600 talents[6] – and clearly the parable uses the fantastic sum to indicate the massive wealth and boundless mercy of this ruler. This is fiction, of course, and the exaggerated sum of 60 million denarii owed to the king by the slave will heighten the impression made on the audience by contrast with the 100 denarii owed to the same slave. More importantly, as M. De Boer points out, Matthew has raised the amount "primarily because the extraordinarily large sum underscores the depth of God's mercy, disclosed in the work of Jesus, to the supplicant and properly worshipful 'debtor' (v 26)".[7]

The first slave cannot pay back the sums he has diverted from the imperial treasury, so the king orders him to be sold, together with his wife and children and all his possessions. Jewish law, which forbade selling fellow Jews into slavery except for theft, does not apply in this case. The absolute monarch's decision to sell the slave and his family, as J.D. Derrett points out, is not a way of recovering the funds but a public punishment for failure to honour the contract.[8] The money realised from the sale of the slave and his family would be nothing beside the huge sum owed. The king, however, must make an example of this failed bureaucrat; the harsher his sentence, the less likely that others will follow suit. He is prepared to exercise power ruthlessly by making the whole family suffer a fate they can never overcome.

The guilty slave prostrates himself before his lord; the verb Matthew uses is *prosekynia* – which, as Linnemann observes, "is in fact usually used in the sense of the worship of God or gods".[9] This may be further evidence of Matthew's allegorising tendency in the parable. In worshipping his lord and begging for mercy, the slave is probably asking the king to forgo the amount for this year, effectively asking his master for a loan. Given his influential position in the kingdom – the bureaucrat is probably a genius at extracting tribute and taxes from the provinces – it is not unlikely that with his contacts and specialised skills, he can manage to pay back a substantial amount of what he owes. Up until this recent failure, he has proved himself a loyal servant of the king, and he has now responded to the king with worshipful desperation.

When the king witnesses his failed bureaucrat on his knees, begging for more time, he is moved with pity and releases the slave from the debt. The king's decision is capricious – arbitrariness is a characteristic of all authoritarian rule, keeping everyone on edge – and it shows his absolute power over the law and his slave. We are given no reason for the king's change of mind: we know only that on a whim he decides to be merciful, releasing the slave from the whole of the enormous debt.

The second reckoning
Having survived a huge personal and family crisis, the reinstated bureaucrat leaves the king's presence a forgiven man. He meets a fellow slave – this *syndoulos* would be a lesser official, not as high-ranking as the first slave. As the king was lord over the first slave, so the first slave is lord over this newcomer on the scene. He adopts the posture of the angry, abused patron who must assert his authority immediately to regain control. He seizes the middle-level bureaucrat by the throat and demands, "Pay what you owe me." The fellow slave falls on his knees and pleads with him, making the same speech as the first slave made earlier to the king. But the first slave refuses to be moved by pity, and throws the lesser mortal into prison until he can pay the debt of one hundred denarii.

The hearer is confused. The story structures us to expect a positive response from the forgiven slave: the king's recent forgiveness, the smallness of the debt, and the bond between fellow servants (*syndoulos auto*), however different their stations, suggest that the first slave will react with kindness.

The first slave owed a tremendous debt that he probably could never have paid fully, and experienced mercy. He was owed a debt of one hundred denarii that could have been paid in time, but he exacted an austere justice. The slave's act seems remarkably stupid and thoughtless. Not only does he fail to connect with the mercy he has just experienced, he clearly fails to anticipate the retaliation that will surely be visited on him. He acts now in the very way that probably made him such an efficient tribute collector, with unyielding violence on those who cannot deliver what is needed.

In trying to understand the slave's behaviour, the clinical psychologist R. Ford comments:

> It may be that his behaviour has little to do with control over his weaker colleague and far more to do with efforts to restore those long-standing patterns of dominance and submission holding him

together with his master. To satisfy his urgent need for continuity, this competent person ignores warnings clamouring for attention, namely, that to survive (through customary deference) he ought immediately to imitate his new master. The slave's need to have his familiar world back may at this moment be more compelling than considering how to remain safe. Safety as an issue can come into focus only when the means of safety can be imagined.

If the master will not continue in the role of master and maintain for his slave the established order – the order which heretofore has contained all of the possibilities for predictability, then the slave ignoring his personal safety, will within his constructed imagination attempt to pull that order back in place. [10]

I think Ford's point is well made. The person that the slave mimics is the master he has always known, not the new, generous master. Probably in all their dealings with people *both the king and the slave* have shown only ruthless control: it is this way, after all, that has secured and maintained their various positions of power. They live in a world that is divided between those who control and those who are controlled, between those who dominate and those who are dominated. Apart from the recent, new experience of being shown mercy, worshipful obeisance to his king or unrelenting dominion over those under him is probably all the bureaucrat knows about the art of relating to people.

In treating his fellow slave as he does, the first slave might be trying to grab back the old familiar way of dealing with people, of rejoining the world that he knows best. This way of acting will also serve to reassert his own authority before others, an authority that has been diminished by falling prostrate on the floor before the king and becoming a beggar for his freedom. In the understanding of the slave, perhaps the unique act of magnanimity shown by the king weighs little against centuries of oppression. Has the king's single act of goodness the power to overthrow centuries of institutionalised abuse? Can the slave leave the practice of domination that has defined his world and move into the world of mercy *that easily*?

None of this is said to justify the slave's behaviour; it is said only to try to understand it, for it does seem puzzling to watch him act so crudely and mercilessly after he has just experienced forgiveness.

The third reckoning

When his fellow slaves see what is happening, they are greatly distressed. Their reaction (*elupaithasan* – they were grieved or sorrowful; *sphodra* – very much, greatly) will stand in dramatic contrast to the master's response of anger (*orgistheis* – being angry, wrathful). The man's fellow slaves are not outraged, but overcome by grief. Perhaps they are aware of the first slave's immediate reversal to type following his forgiveness; perhaps they see that this man was simply out of control, acting out the need to make someone pay for the confusion he has experienced; perhaps they simply identify with their imprisoned colleague. Whatever, it is grief not outrage that leads them not to confront their colleague about his behaviour but to appeal directly to the king.

I think their reaction is important in the sequence of the story. In doing what they do, they illustrate what Matthew *argues against* earlier in this chapter: that when your brother offends you, "go and point out the fault when the two of you are alone. If the member listens to you, you have regained that one. But if you are not listened to, take one or two others along with you, so that every word may be confirmed by the evidence of two or three witnesses" (Mt 18:15-16). Why do the slaves not confront their fellow slave? Why do they appeal directly to the ultimate hierarchical figure in the person of the king? Did they in their grief imagine that he would settle the whole affair in his new mood of mercy? We are not told why they go directly to the king. Had they confronted their fellow slave themselves, there would have been a possibility for the whole thing to be settled informally and quietly. Their action dramatically illustrates the danger of appealing to hierarchy to settle a dispute among fellow employees.

The king summons the first slave, addresses him briefly and immediately delivers a judgement: "'You wicked slave! I forgave you all that debt because you pleaded with me. Should you not have had mercy on your fellow slave, as I had mercy on you?' And in anger his lord handed him over to be tortured until he would pay his entire debt" (Mt 18:32-34). The king's speech states what the hearer of the parable believes: that the slave must (*dei*) behave as the king did, that the mercy he was shown obliged him to be merciful himself. In this understanding, pity is not something you feel, it is a duty you are obliged to share. If the patron shows mercy, so the client is obliged to follow suit: it was not just a personal beneficence, but was for the good of the kingdom that the king showed mercy to this slave. In failing to take his cue from his lord, in refusing to multiply such kindness in the kingdom, the slave has shamed his patron and violated his honour. He has forced his patron to revert to type, to business as usual. And in doing that the slave will pay a terrible price.

The harshness of the punishment finds the king going back on his original word: he withdraws his forgiveness and reinstates the original debt. The last case is worse than the first: the first punishment for the slave was being sold into slavery, the final punishment is never-ending torture. While torture was forbidden in Jewish law, Herod the Great and his sons employed it, as did most governments in antiquity. No amount of torture, of course, would enable the slave to pay back the immense amount that he owed.

The last line of the parable is obviously Matthew's addition: Matthew cannot believe that God retains a corps of torturers to deal with unforgiving members of the Christian community. Matthew's point, however, is well made: the unforgivable sin in the Christian community is to be unforgiving.

Reflection

The parable ends in chaotic retribution as the king goes back on his word, reverts to type and commands the torture of the slave until he can repay the whole debt. Given the colossal size of the debt, given that the slave will be incarcerated and tortured in prison, the sentence has the touch of the eternal about it. Whatever else the king is, he is no figure of God. He is manifestly incapable of transferring the mercy he has shown earlier to his bureaucratic machine. As W.R. Herzog comments: "The functionaries had internalised the system to such an extent that they were creatures of it. The systematic dynamics of the bureaucracy alone would force the cancellation of forgiveness and any other policy that threatened the existence of the bureaucracy itself."[11] The king is caught within his own cycle of power politics: no sooner has the new age of forgiveness begun than it is cancelled by the vengeful tactics of the one who inaugurated it.

Whatever else the slaves intended when they appealed to the king to settle the matter, their action has brought chaos to the story. The parable finishes with the hearers themselves being caught in the trap of their own devising, when they agreed with the slaves to petition the king. All told, it is a very untidy ending to a story that began in such a promising way with the dispensation of mercy.

B.B. Scott comments on the feeling the parable leaves the reader with: "A hearer is entrapped in a web of evil that results from the attempt to bring justice, or what the hearer and fellow servants judge to be justice . . . The narrative leads to a parabolic experience of evil, not intentional evil but implicit, unanticipated, systematic evil. The ability to acknowledge one's entanglement in evil is part of the experience of the kingdom."[12] One feels caught inside the parable, precisely because the parable enticed the readers to make their own judgements about how the process should continue after the second reckoning, when the first slave threw the other slave into prison. In agreeing with the other slaves to report the matter to the king, one then sees the result of that judgement in the slave's consignment to prison and his punishment of torture. Who wants that? By then, of course, it is too late to go back, it is too late to reshape the story by following Matthew's earlier advice: When one of your brothers sins against you, go and have it out with him alone.

It seems to me that Matthew is using the parable, among other things, to illustrate the folly of appealing to hierarchy as a way of solving problems. In the parable the appeal to hierarchy ends up with chaos reigning. If the grieving slaves had exercised *their own leadership* in confronting the first slave, if they had pointed out to him how profoundly unfair his treatment of his fellow slave was, then there might have been a different ending. At least there would have been the opportunity for the slave to change his mind. But that conversation never happened.

Without that conversation, the appeal to hierarchy results in a final judgement that has no higher court of appeal, whereas Matthew's formula for handling conflict deliberately has a graded approach to it, with three stages of appeal: first by the individual who is offended, then by a group of two or three, and finally by the community. That approach is not used, and the results are disastrous. Thus in the parable everyone loses: the king, the first slave, the second slave, and the slaves who appealed to the king.

One can only wonder what would have happened if the participants in the story had followed the advice of Matthew? What would have happened if the slaves had exercised their own leadership in the community, taken responsibility for their own fellow slave, and together confronted him? According to Matthew's values if everyone in the Christian community does not exercise his or her responsibility for leadership of the community, unless people take their own authority for ensuring the values of the community are lived out, then the final court of appeal will be the first and the last stop for those who have sinned. That, Matthew believes, is a recipe for disaster.

[1] J.P. Meier, *Matthew,* p.200

[2] R.E. Brown, *The Churches the Apostles Left Behind*, p.145

[3] K. Whitelam, "King and Kingship" in *The Anchor Bible Dictionary* Vol 4, p.40

[4] T. Carney, *The Shape of the Past: Models and Antiquity,* pp. 63, 90

[5] T. Carney, *The Shape of the Past: Models and Antiquity*, p. 52

[6] Josephus, *Antiquities* 17.11.4

[7] M. De Boer, "Ten Thousand Talents? Matthew's Interpretation and Redaction of the Parable of the Unforgiving Servant" in *Catholic Biblical Quarterly* 50 (1988) p.228

[8] J.D. Derrett, *Law in the New Testament,* p.37

[9] E. Linnemann, *Jesus of the Parables,* p.109

[10] R. Ford, *The Parables of Jesus*, p.51

[11] W.R. Herzog, *Parables as Subversive Speech*, p.148

[12] B.B. Scott, *Hear Then the Parable*, p.280

Introduction: Luke 15:1-3 (NRSV)

¹Now all the tax collectors and sinners were coming near to listen to him. ² And the Pharisees and the scribes were grumbling and saying, "This fellow welcomes sinners and eats with them." ³ So he told them this parable.

The context

The three parables in chapter 15 of Luke, stories of simple beauty and compassionate outreach, have often been called "the heart of the Gospel". Luke gathers them together to celebrate Jesus' love for the last and the least and the lost, while noting how that joyful commitment brings him into open confrontation with the religious authorities. Luke sets the context by contrasting the difference between Jesus' hearers, two separate groups, and the reasons they come into his presence:

➢ *Tax collectors and sinners*   *come near to him*   *to listen to him*
➢ *Pharisees and scribes*   *come*   *to complain*

The audience is made up of the outcasts and the outraged. The outcasts are named as tax collectors and sinners, and from the earliest strata of the Gospel tradition Jesus is associated in table fellowship with them. Who were the tax collectors? John Donahue, in his study of this group,[1] argues that the earliest usage of tax collectors in the Greek city states and the Roman empire describes those who purchased the right to collect taxes: they would pay the state in advance the sum to be collected and manage their own profit from the actual sum they collected. This abusive practice was drastically curtailed first by Julius Caesar and then by Augustus. By the time of Herod the Great, royal officials connected directly to the centre of government collected the direct taxes – the poll tax and the land tax. Under the Roman prefects, officials employed by the Romans had responsibility for gathering the direct taxes. Similarly in Galilee, the tax collectors were under the direct authority of Herod Antipas.

Added to the direct taxes were a number of indirect taxes, especially on the transport of goods. (Jews were obliged to pay religious taxes such as the Temple tax and the tithes on produce to support the Jerusalem priests.) Collection of indirect taxes was subcontracted to employees of tax officials, who could be Jewish citizens. It is these *toll* collectors, who appear at commercial centres such as Capernaum and Jericho, with whom Jesus associates in the Gospels. Because of the nature of their job they were popularly regarded as dishonest people whose work made it unlikely that they would ever repent; given the exorbitant tariffs they charged, they were clearly engaged in lucrative arithmetic for their own benefit. The principal reason Jesus causes scandal is because he associates with people who are patently dishonest and disreputable, such as toll collectors, people who live outside the Law in a blatant manner.

The term "sinners" refers not only to those who are regarded as leading immoral lives but also those whose trade put them beyond the boundary of religious or social approval. As J. Jeremias noted: "The term 'sinners' means: (1) People who led an immoral life (e.g. adulterers, swindlers) and (2) people who followed a dishonourable calling (i.e. an occupation which notoriously involved immorality or dishonesty), and who were on that account deprived of civil rights, such as holding office, or bearing witness in legal proceedings. For example, excise-men, tax collectors, donkey-drivers, pedlars and tanners."[2] The Pharisees express their disapproval that in consorting and eating with these people, Jesus is engaging in irreligious behaviour.

The Pharisees – the "separated ones" – come to complain about Jesus' pastoral strategy of associating with sinners: "This fellow welcomes sinners and eats with them." The Pharisees and scribes have already registered their objection at the house of Levi, and the similarities to the present scene are striking:

Luke 5:29-30	*Luke 15:1-2*
a great crowd	all
tax collectors and others	tax collectors and sinners
the Pharisees and scribes	the Pharisees and scribes
were complaining	were grumbling
Why eat with tax collectors and sinners?	He welcomes sinners and eats with them

At the house of Levi Jesus defends himself not through parable but through voicing what could be considered his mission statement: "I have come to call not the righteous but sinners to repentance" (Lk 5:32). Later, in drawing a contrast between himself and John the Baptist, Jesus notes the difference between John's ascetic lifestyle and his own: "For John the Baptist has come eating no bread and drinking no wine, and you say, 'He has a demon'; the Son of Man has come eating and drinking, and you say, 'Look a glutton and a drunkard, a friend of tax collectors and sinners!'" (Lk 7:33-34). Jesus' pastoral strategy of associating with sinners at table has provoked his critics to caricature him as a hedonist.

Both Jesus and the Pharisees believed in fellowship meals. The Pharisees believed, like many others, that sharing a meal meant fellowship with God and with those who shared the blessings of God. To break bread with others was to accept them, to offer them fellowship, to honour them, make a sanctuary for them, and share life with them. To share your table with the unclean and the wicked was considered an openly sacrilegious act. For the Pharisees, as for the majority of religious people, the conversion of sinners was a necessary *precondition* for table fellowship.

Jesus' genius is to reverse the sequence: he uses the meal *as a way of coming to fellowship with him prior to conversion*. Zacchaeus' conversion, for example, is not a condition for eating with Jesus; rather table fellowship with Jesus is what leads to Zacchaeus' change (Lk 19:1-10). Jesus' pastoral strategy is built on respect rather than on threat: in associating with tax collectors and sinners, Jesus is clearly affirming their basic worth before God – which is why the Pharisees and the scribes object so strongly. Jesus does not believe that keeping sinners isolated, making them feel like moral lepers, is likely to lead to their conversion; it is far more likely to confirm them in moral paralysis. Love and forgiveness are offered in the hope that change and renewal will be the outcome; love and forgiveness are not, therefore, a reward for conversion.

The sequence of forgiveness leading to conversion is celebrated in the Wisdom of Solomon. Not surprisingly, the insight begins with the image of a merciful God:

> But you are merciful to all, for you can do all things,
> and you overlook people's sins, so that they may repent.
> For you love all things that exist
> and detest none of the things you have made,
> for you would not have made anything if you had hated it.
> How would anything have endured if you had not willed it?
> Or how would anything not called forth by you have been preserved?

You spare all things,
for they are yours, O Lord, you who love the living.
For your immortal spirit is in all things.
Therefore you correct little by little those who trespass,
and you remind and warn them of the things through which they sin,
so that they may be freed from wickedness
and put their trust in you, O Lord.   (Wis 11:23 – 12:2)

Jesus' pastoral strategy emerges from the *kind of God* he believes in. Jesus' readiness to forgive, to break bread, to seek out those who live beyond the boundaries of religious and social approval – all this is a commentary on the kind of God he believes in. When his preference for the outcast meets the outrage of the righteous, Jesus confronts the religious values of his opponents. By cherishing the people they despise, Jesus calls into question the value system that allows religious people to ignore and rubbish others and the kind of God that supports that destructive attitude. As T.W. Manson notes: "The root of the matter is that it is God himself who wills that the outcast should be gathered in. The attitude of Jesus to publicans and sinners is not a mere humanitarian enthusiasm on his part: it is the manifestation of the will and purpose of God. The scribes and Pharisees cannot accept that without qualification."[3]

By way of confronting Jesus' accusers and their pastoral strategy of separation, Luke gives us three parables that act as a defence for Jesus' own practice of associating with sinners and then welcoming them unconditionally into table fellowship:

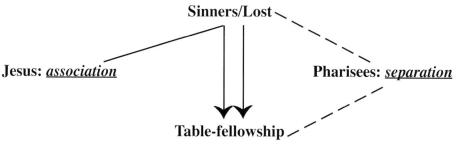

The three parables, which have their own separate characters and plots, are united in their theme of vindicating Jesus' pastoral strategy and are held together by key human moments – the experience of loss, the experience of finding again, the joy of rediscovery shared with others. The focus in each parable is on the character that has experienced the loss, and on his/her commitment and energy to be reunited with the lost one. In all three parables the loss is important, just as the loss of sinners is important to Jesus, which is why the introductory verses play such an important part for Luke in clarifying the purpose of each of the parables.

The Lost Sheep: Luke 15:4-7

4"Which one of you, having a hundred sheep and losing one of them, does not leave the ninety-nine in the wilderness and go after the one that is lost until he finds it? 5When he has found it, he lays it on his shoulders and rejoices. 6And when he comes home, he calls together his friends and neighbours, saying to them, 'Rejoice with me, for I have found my sheep that was lost.' 7Just so, I tell you, there will be more joy in heaven over one sinner who repents than over ninety-nine righteous persons who need no repentance."

Matthew 18:12-14

12"What do you think? If a shepherd has a hundred sheep, and one of them has gone astray, does he not leave the ninety-nine on the mountains and go in search of the one that went astray? 13 And if he finds it, truly, I tell you, he rejoices over it more than over the ninety-nine that never went astray. 14 So it is not the will of your Father in heaven that one of these little ones should be lost."

Gospel of Thomas 107

Jesus said, "The kingdom is like a shepherd who has a hundred sheep. One of them, which was the largest, went astray. He left the ninety-nine behind and looked for the one until he found it. Having tired himself out, he said to the sheep, 'I care for you more than the ninety-nine.'"

The parable of The Lost Sheep is the only one in Luke 15 that has a Synoptic parallel, in Matthew 18:12-14. While Matthew and Luke both preserve the parable in the form of a question, *Thomas* has the parable as a simile: "The kingdom is like . . ." In the versions of Matthew and *Thomas* the sheep goes astray of its own volition, whereas Luke notes that the shepherd has lost one sheep and goes after it, and announces on his return that he has found it. In *Thomas* the lost sheep is identified as the largest, which is probably a reference back to Ezekiel 34:16.[4]

Also there is no rejoicing, but the sheep is addressed directly by Jesus and its worth affirmed.

It is difficult to assess whether the version of Matthew or Luke is the more original. It is probably wiser to see each evangelist adapting the story from his source to his own editorial needs: Matthew is addressing Christian leaders, urging them not to despise little ones; Luke is describing a confrontation between Jesus and the Pharisees over their differing pastoral strategies towards the lost. Each evangelist adapts Jesus' story about the lost sheep to further his own theological purposes.

Luke's parable begins by a direct appeal to the Pharisees and the scribes to imagine themselves as a shepherd who has the unfortunate experience of losing one of his hundred sheep. Shepherds belonged to a proscribed trade – they were considered to be dishonest and thieving – and thus were categorised as unclean and as sinners. Jesus asks the Pharisees to consider themselves as sinners: "Which of you, having a hundred sheep . . .?" Jesus is effectively inviting the Pharisees to put themselves in the position of the very sinner from whom they remain staunchly separated.

The traditional biblical imagery of shepherd/flock probably derives from Israel's earliest years of nomadic existence. From the very beginning the first two brothers, Cain and Abel, the farmer and the shepherd, with their different work and values, are seen as rivals:

Farmer	**Shepherd**
Cain	Abel
landed	nomadic
crops	animals
plot of land	open space
settler	pioneer
security	freedom
stay at home	wandering

While the shepherd is the heroic image of a nomadic people, that image changed when the people became landed and adapted themselves to an agricultural and urban economy. The tradition of Israel's nomadic life in the desert seems to have given rise to the image of God as their shepherd and protector (Gen 48:15; 49:24).

God's devotion and loyalty to an individual sheep is celebrated in the classic Shepherd Psalm (23). Israel's leaders were often regarded as shepherds, which originally some of them were, like Moses, Saul, and David. The symbol of shepherd as leader receives its most extensive treatment in Ezekiel 34, where the prophet uses the evil shepherd theme to illustrate irresponsible leadership. By the first century, however, shepherds were regarded as unclean and a threat to the property of the landed. As J.D. Derrett observed: "The shepherd was despised socially on account of his flocks' eating private property, whatever prestige the occupation of shepherd might have in the eyes of allegorists."[5]

The format of Luke's story runs as follows:

having ⟹ losing ⟹ searching ⟹ finding

restoring with joy ⟹ rejoicing in community

The story opens in crisis with a shepherd, after counting the sheep, realising that he has lost one of them. (The first Dead Sea scrolls were discovered by a shepherd who, having failed to count his flock the previous evening, counted them at 11 am and noticed that a goat was missing.) Even though the shepherd in the parable has ninety-nine safely at hand, the loss of one sheep still matters to him. He does not write off the missing sheep as a lost cause; he does not sit down in the wilderness and mourn its loss, but goes off in search of the lost one. The loss is registered as important, so the search begins. Search is not automatic after loss; only if the loss is registered as important do we seek out what is lost. As the saying goes, "Where there is no love there is no loss." The imagery is similar to that used by Ezekiel: "I myself will search for my sheep, and will seek them out . . . I will seek the lost, and I will bring back the strayed" (Ez 34:11, 16).

The shepherd leaves the ninety-nine sheep behind him in the wilderness. B.B. Scott argues that "Matthew and Luke clearly imply that the ninety-nine are abandoned."[6] I think it is more likely that the evangelists' silence about the ninety-nine reflects their chosen focus on how the shepherd immediately reacts to the fact that he has lost one sheep. Besides, it is highly improbable that one shepherd would have responsibility for so many sheep. As N. Levison, who grew up in a Middle East village, points out: "I have never seen in Syria, Palestine or Mesopotamia a flock attended by a single person. Two, and even three, shepherds are commonly employed. When one sheep is lost and the shepherd goes to seek it, the other shepherd takes the flock home."[7] It is also worth noting that the shepherd on his return would hardly call his friends and neighbours to rejoice that he had found one lost sheep if he had left the other ninety-nine abandoned in the wilderness.

The sheep is lost in the middle of the wilderness, not among fenced fields, so the looking has to be serious, over crags and among rocks and crevices, and it continues until the shepherd finds the lost one. When he finds it, the real work begins, for he has to shoulder the weight of the frightened sheep and make his way back through the rocky wilderness to home. But when he lays the weight of the sheep on his shoulders, the shepherd rejoices: his joy is greater than the burden of restoration he has to endure. That joy is intact at journey's end when the shepherd wants to share it with his friends and neighbours: "Rejoice with me, for I have found the sheep that was lost." The clear implication is that the sheep is restored to the fold now gathered in the village.

After the story, the teaching shifts to repentance, with Jesus saying, "There will be more joy in heaven over one sinner who repents than over ninety-nine righteous persons who have no need of repentance." The focus of joy is no longer the finding of a lost sheep but the return of a repentant sinner. How does the parable illustrate repentance, which is usually considered a precondition for forgiveness? The sheep does not actually do anything, apart from getting lost and being found. As G. Bornkamm observes: "So little is repentance a human action preparing the way for grace, that it can be placed on the same level as being found."[8] The focus in the parable fastens onto what the responsible shepherd does in his compassionate outreach; it is *he* who assumes the burden of responsibility for reinstating the lost one. And he does all this with joy. The emphasis on joy after anxiety and loss unites the three parables and adds to their depth of meaning.

Even though the sheep was lost, the shepherd saw the lost one as still belonging to him; that connection was never severed through the sheep's being lost. That the shepherd should go to such trouble to search for one per cent of his property emphasises the depth of feeling impelling him. Given Luke's setting of the parable, the clear inference is that the tax collectors and sinners, despite being lost and despite being rejected by the Pharisees and the scribes, still belong to God, and that God himself seeks to bring them back safely to the fold. This, for Luke, is what God is seen to be doing through the person of Jesus: "For the Son of Man came to seek out and to save the lost" (Lk 19:10).

The Lost Coin: Luke 15:8-10

[8]*"Or what woman having ten silver coins, if she loses one of them, does not light a lamp, sweep the house, and search carefully until she finds it?* [9]*When she has found it, she calls together her friends and neighbours, saying, 'Rejoice with me, for I have found the coin that I had lost.'* [10]*Just so, I tell you, there is joy in the presence of the angels of God over one sinner who repents."*

The parable of The Lost Coin emerges as a twin to the parable of The Lost Sheep. Both parables are in the form of a rhetorical question, and the structure between the two is immediately striking and can be seen in their parallel lines:

The Lost Sheep	The Lost Coin
Which man of you,	Or what woman,
having a hundred sheep,	having ten silver coins,
and losing one of them,	if she loses one of them,
does not leave . . .	does not light . . .
until he finds it?	until she finds it?
When he has found it . . .	When she has found it . . .
he calls together	she calls together
his friends and neighbours,	her friends and neighbours,
saying to them,	saying,
Rejoice with me,	Rejoice with me,
for I have found my sheep	for I have found the coin
that was lost.	that I had lost.
Just so, I tell you,	Just so, I tell you,
there will be more joy . . .	there is joy . . .
over one sinner who repents . . .	over one sinner who repents.

To invite the Pharisees to accept the woman in the parable as their teacher, as to accept the shepherd in the previous parable, is going beyond what was socially and religiously acceptable. The twin parables play on the contrast between a man and a woman. As B. Witherington notes: "But this contrast is meant neither to disparage either role, nor to elevate one above the other as more important; rather, it illustrates in a pointed fashion that both the activity of the man and the woman are equally admirable and important, and may equally well serve as analogies for the activity of God in Jesus' ministry."[9]

The parable of The Lost Coin is carried forward by the dramatic progression of the woman's verbs: she *loses*, she *lights* a lamp, she *sweeps* the house, she *searches* carefully, she *calls* together her friends and neighbours, and *asks* them *to rejoice* with her. As in the previous parable, what began as an individual loss, moving on to unwearied search, ends with community rejoicing.

The woman loses a *drachma*, the only time this word is used in the New Testament. It was a Greek silver coin equal in value to the denarius, and in the parable it is one of ten. J. Jeremias has suggested that the ten coins could have been part of the woman's dowry and worn as a decorative head-dress.[10] If so, she was poor and her diligent search for the coin is understandable. She begins her search by lighting a lamp: the window in her dwelling is small, to keep out wind and rain, and it admits little light. Then she sweeps the house, probably using a broom made from palm leaves, hoping that the gleam of the coin or its sound against the rock or hardened dirt floor would alert her to its presence. When she finds it, her reaction to being reunited with her lost coin is so great that she cannot keep her joy to herself: in spite of her poverty, she feels compelled to call in her friends and neighbours to join her in celebration.

The conclusion drawn is similar to that of the previous parable. If someone will stubbornly search for their lost property, however trivial it may seem, until it is found, how much more care will God take to secure the return of those who are lost. In both parables, the joy that seeks to share itself in community is seen as utterly natural. Are the Pharisees and the scribes among those who delight that the lost have now been found? In both parables the argument is simply expounded: granted that it is God's desire and plan that the lost should be saved, then Jesus' pastoral strategy of associating with sinners is fully justified because it earths God's redeeming activity.

The Lost Sons: Luke 15:11-32

[11]*Then Jesus said, "There was a man who had two sons.* [12] *The younger of them said to his father, 'Father, give me the share of the property that will belong to me.' So he divided his property between them.* [13]*A few days later the younger son gathered all he had and travelled to a distant country, and there he squandered his property in dissolute living.*

[14]*"When he had spent everything, a severe famine took place throughout that country and he began to be in need.* [15]*So he went and hired himself out to one of*

132

the citizens of that country, who sent him to his fields to feed the pigs. ¹⁶ He would gladly have filled himself with the pods that the pigs were eating; and no one gave him anything. ¹⁷But when he came to himself he said, 'How many of my father's hired hands have bread enough and to spare, but here I am dying of hunger! ¹⁸I will get up and go to my father, and I will say to him, "Father, I have sinned against heaven and before you; ¹⁹I am no longer worthy to be called your son; treat me like one of your hired hands."'

²⁰*"So he set off and went to his father. But while he was still far off, his father saw him and was filled with compassion; he ran and put his arms around him and kissed him. ²¹Then the son said to him, 'Father, I have sinned against heaven and before you; I am no longer worthy to be called your son.' ²²But the father said to his slaves, 'Quickly, bring out a robe – the best one – and put it on him; put a ring on his finger and sandals on his feet. ²³And get the fatted calf and kill it, and let us eat and celebrate; ²⁴for this son of mine was dead and is alive again; he was lost and is found!' And they began to celebrate.*

²⁵*"Now his elder son was in the field; and when he came and approached the house, he heard music and dancing. ²⁶He called one of the slaves and asked what was going on. ²⁷He replied, 'Your brother has come, and your father has killed the fatted calf, because he has got him back safe and sound.' ²⁸Then he became angry and refused to go in. His father came out and began to plead with him. ²⁹But he answered his father, 'Listen! For all these years I have been working like a slave for you, and I have never disobeyed your command; yet you have never given me even a young goat so that I might celebrate with my friends. ³⁰But when this son of yours came back, who has devoured your property with prostitutes, you killed the fatted calf for him!' ³¹Then the father said to him, 'Son, you are always with me, and all that is mine is yours. ³²But we had to celebrate and rejoice, because this brother of yours was dead and has come to life; he was lost and has been found.'"*

The social context

The parable of The Father and Two Sons, traditionally called The Prodigal Son, tells the story of a father who has two sons and who loses both of them: the younger one is lost in a far country, while the elder is lost in the wilderness of his own self-righteous hostility. One leaves home in the fond hope that he will find happiness in the world of the unfamiliar only to discover that it is found at the heart of the familiar. One stays at home, but he seems such a stranger to the love and joy which surround him that he might as well be an alien in a foreign land. They are a mixed human family in which tenderness and selfishness and hostility all vie with each other for possession. By the end of the story, tenderness has won over selfishness, but it is unclear if hostility will remain out in the cold.

The parable tells the story of a family quarrel, which is initiated by the younger son's request for his share of the property. In the ancient Mediterranean world the family, not the individual, was the primary unit of importance and the psychological centre of life. Who you were was determined by your position in the family and the regard they and others had for you. Identity was family identity, not personal identity; individualism was shunned in favour of family loyalty. As R. Rohrbaugh comments:

> Family members are deeply embedded in each other socially, economically and psychologically, hence the loyalty they owe to one another is simply categorical. They watch each other constantly for hints that kin-group loyalty is weak and any member acting outside the pattern of the family is deeply resented. When describing a family celebration, for example, the first-century Roman poet Ovid puts it bluntly, "Let the innocent appear; let the disloyal brother stay far, far away." Interestingly, Ovid counts among the "disloyal" any brother with an excessive interest in inheriting the property, that is, "anyone who thinks his father is still too much alive."[11]

If family solidarity was the primary social value in the ancient Mediterranean world, solidarity with the village came a close second. In a world where few people travelled beyond the reach of the nearest market town, the family and the village set the geographical and emotional boundaries of the majority of people. In the tightly knit community of the village, where you lived your life in close proximity to relations and neighbours, social conformity was a matter of survival, an essential part of maintaining self-esteem and "respect" within the close network of relations. Who you were was determined to a large extent not on how you regarded yourself but on how you were regarded in the eyes of your fellow villagers, whether you commanded their respect or not.

For example, when Jesus returns to his own village after his time with John the

Baptist, he appears as a prophetic teacher, as someone now different from the one who left the village. His fellow villagers are astounded: "They said, 'Where did this man get all this? What is this wisdom that has been given to him? Is not this the carpenter, the son of Mary and brother of James and Joses and Judas and Simon, and are not his sisters here with us?' And they took offence at him" (Mk 6:2-3). The villagers quickly move from noticing what is new, the wisdom of Jesus, to focusing on what they already know about him – his job and his relatives – and it is the latter recognition that constitutes for them the real identity of Jesus. He is, after all, Jesus *of Nazareth*. The people of Nazareth cannot accept the Jesus who has now returned to the village as a changed man.

Jesus is rejected by his own people because he does not conform to their local expectations; in their eyes he has become a non-conformist. As M. Diaz writes: "Characteristically, in the peasant community, where the nonconformity of one is frequently seen as a threat to the cohesion of the whole, the limits are very narrow. The individual wishing to maintain viable face-to-face relations with his fellow villagers finds that he must play the game according to local rules."[12] Jesus refuses to play by those rules and it is not surprising that in the Gospel narrative he never returns to his own village again.

Central to family identity was its relationship to land. In Israel the *bêt'-ab* ("father's house") was the basic kinship structure that provided the individual with his/her sense of inclusion, identity and responsibility. The "father's house" was the extended family which included the head of the house and his wife, his sons and their wives (married daughters joined their husbands' *bêt'-ab*), his grandsons and their wives, plus any unmarried sons and daughters, along with dependants such as slaves and resident labourers. C. Wright comments on the family's relationship to land:

> The *bêt'-ab* was the basic unit of Israel's system of land tenure, each having its own inheritance of land, and therewith intended to be economically self-sufficient. The intention of Israel's land tenure system, namely that ownership of land should be as widely spread as possible with broad equality over the network of economically viable units, was embodied in and protected by the principle of *inalienability*. This was the rule that the land should remain in the family to which it had been apportioned, and could not be sold

permanently outside the family. It was a rule tenaciously adhered to throughout Israel's history, as far as the evidence points. The whole Old Testament gives us no single example of an Israelite voluntarily selling land outside his family.[13]

The selling of family land was not only an economic tragedy but also a social disaster: it meant diminishment of the family resources together with loss of honour and place in the eyes of the villagers. Traditionally there was an expectation that a kinsman would buy the land in order to keep it within the family network (Lev 25:25). In selling their own land members of the family were seen to be selling themselves and their honour, and it is this problem that opens the parable of The Father and Two Sons.

The division of the property

The parable opens with a brief introduction to the three characters who will play their part in the drama, a man and his two sons. The younger son initiates the plot of the parable by requesting his father for the share of the family property that should fall to him. As K.E. Bailey has pointed out,[14] together with a number of commentators, the younger son's request is tantamount to wishing his father dead. Ben Sirach argues forcefully against a father doing this; he does not even contemplate a son requesting it:

> To son or wife, to brother or friend,
> do not give power over yourself, as long as you live;
> and do not give your property to another,
> in case you change your mind and must ask for it.
> While you are still alive and have breath in you,
> do not let anyone take your place.
> For it is better that your children should ask from you
> than that you should look to the hand of your children.
> Excel in all that you do;
> bring no stain upon your honour.
> At the time when you end the days of your life,
> in the hour of death, distribute your inheritance. (Sir 33:20-24)

According to Ben Sirach, the father is utterly foolhardy in granting the request of his younger son. Not only that, but in a world where the primary social value is the solidarity with the family and with the village, the father is endangering his own reputation by bringing a "stain" on his honour. In dividing his property among his two sons, he is flaunting traditional values and custom, and other families in the village would probably close ranks against him lest they be affected by his shameless example.

None of the family emerges unscathed from this opening scene. The younger son requests his portion of the substance (*ousia*) and the narrator remarks that the father responds by dividing his life (*bios*) between his two sons. The younger son's selfish request leads the father to give away not just his livelihood but his life. In agreeing without protest to do this, the father jeopardises the family honour in the eyes of others. And in not protesting about what is happening, but in receiving, instead, his own share of the property, the elder brother is culpable of standing by while his family breaks up.

The younger son receives the right not only of possession of his share in the inheritance but the right of disposal, and within a matter of days he sells his portion, gathers all he has, and travels to a distant country. His portion of land was designed for the opposite reason – to keep the family land intact and to keep the son attached to his family and his village. In selling the land and retaining the money for his own use, the younger son has greatly diminished the support the land offers to the extended family. The elder son would have received two-thirds of the property (see Dt 21:17 where the firstborn by right receives a double portion of the inheritance). The elder son thus becomes the sole owner of what remains of the father's estate, although his father retains the right to enjoy the produce (Lk 15:22, 29). In disposing of his portion the younger son forfeits any further right to the estate.

The younger son's journey

In the biblical narrative, as in fairy tales, the youngest son is usually favoured by fortune and ends up inheriting the kingdom: Moses is the younger brother of Aaron, and David and Solomon are youngest sons. In the story of the patriarchs the younger son is often regarded as the favourite: this can be seen in the stories of Cain and Abel, Ishmael and Isaac, Esau and Jacob, and above all in the story of Joseph, the youngest son of Jacob before the birth of Benjamin. The story of Joseph begins with the youngest son who goes to a far country where there is a famine. Joseph is thought to be dead (Gen 37:33) and the means of family reunion is a severe famine (Gen 41:57). Joseph, rejected by his brothers, receives an honoured welcome from the Pharaoh: "Removing his signet ring from his hand, Pharaoh put it on Joseph's hand; he arranged him in garments of fine linen, and put a gold chain around his neck" (Gen 41:42). When the family escapes the scourge of famine, there is the moving meeting between the son and the father: "Joseph made ready his chariot and went up to meet his father Israel in Goshen. He presented himself to him, fell on his neck, and wept on his neck a good while" (Gen 46:29). These roles will be reversed in Luke's parable.

Whereas Isaac, Jacob and Joseph make good in their respective stories, the younger son in the parable, after ensuring there is large distance between himself and his father's house, scatters the money accrued from his property. We are not given any details about his "dissolute living", the elder brother, without the benefit of meeting his younger sibling and hearing his story, describes it as devouring the property "with prostitutes" (15:30). Whatever the details of the younger son's dissipated lifestyle in a far country, it is clearly self-destructive.

When the younger son runs out of money, he runs into a severe famine; the combination of these two events is degrading and deadly. Although he is responsible for his fate, he is not responsible for the famine. Any first-century audience would have feared the scourge of famine; furthermore, a lone Jew in a foreign country, without either family or funds to support him, would attract an audience's sympathy. The younger son's dream of freedom has evaporated; his promised land has become barren; now, a destitute outsider, he is reduced to living as a refugee and a migrant worker.

In his desperation the younger son seeks patronage from "one of the citizens of that country". He is literally "joined to" the citizen (the root of the verb, *kallao*, is *kolla*, or glue). Since citizens were attached to the city, this landowner is presumably an urbanite of some wealth who, even in time of famine, can afford to hire labourers. As G. Foster comments on the relationship between the peasant and the city: "Peasants know they need the city, as an outlet for their surplus production and as the source of many material and nonmaterial items they cannot themselves produce. Yet they recognise that the city is the source of their helplessness and humiliation, and in spite of the patrons half trusted, the peasant knows he can never really count on a city man."[15] Clearly the younger cannot count on his new patron: "no one gave him anything".

As a Jew he engages in the humiliating and forbidden occupation of feeding pigs, and he ends up jealous of the pigs he is attending, for they have carob beans to eat.

More than any other information, the detail about his feeding pigs indicates how completely lost he is: lost to religious, racial and family loyalties. His desperation is so great that he ends up longing to have a share in the pigs' food. Feeding the pigs, he waits passively to be fed himself, but no one pays attention to his need. The animals receive more attention than this wretched human being. The younger son ends up no better than an animal – in a pigpen, longing to be fed with pigs' food.

The story of the son's restoration begins when he comes to himself, when he realises the hopelessness of his present situation. After a long journey and a multitude of experiences, the younger son eventually arrives at himself. Everything has turned out a grotesque failure. The experience of failure forms the *krisis*, the turning point in the story of the younger son. He does not become paralysed in vain regret but resolves to change the situation. In the midst of failure he sees a way out: his memory saves him, allowing him to imagine a future that is different from his destitute present. Remembering how well the hired servants at home are fed, with bread to spare, he contrasts that memory with awareness of his present plight, "but here I am dying of hunger". The younger son resolves to return to the person whom he has abandoned, his father, and to make his confession to him. The hope of reconciliation, not restoration, brings him home.

There is a progressive psychological development in the younger son's story:

> ***A Urge to pursue independent life away from home***
> ***B Requests share of property from father***
> ***C Travels to a far country and loses everything***
> ***D Awareness of hopelessness of his situation***
> ***E Comes to himself in experience of failure***
> ***D¹ Remembering home, making new future possible***
> ***C¹ Returns home and gains everything in father's welcome***
> ***B¹ Requests forgiveness from father***
> ***A¹ Welcomed home to a celebration***

In the structure of development there is a parallelism and antithesis between the various parts of the story. His original urge to pursue an independent life away from home is balanced by the welcome home; the selfish request for his share in the property is balanced by his later request for forgiveness; his losing everything in a far country is reversed by his gaining back his sonship from his father; his awareness of his hopeless situation is saved by his expectation of a kinder future. The experience of failure forms the pivotal point of the story, while the celebration forms its climax.

The younger son rehearses his confession: "Father, I have sinned against heaven and before you; I am no longer worthy to be called your son; treat me like one of your hired hands." He acknowledges that he has sinned not only against God but also against his father – in this confession there is no allegorical equation of the father with God. As part of his admission of failure and sin he includes a proposition, that his father treat him as a hired servant. Believing he has forfeited the right of sonship, the younger son hopes that if he is employed as a hired servant he may be able to pay back what he has lost in an alien land. That act of restoration is part of his repentance; it also arranges for his own survival in the community. Living independently in the village as a hired worker – not being dependent on his brother's hospitality – the younger son seeks to earn the favour of his father. He will still have to face the anger of the villagers, of course, for having treated his father so badly, sold the land, and now lost everything.

He carries out his resolve and leaves the country where his dreams turned into nightmare. Again the parable notes that his destination is the person of his father, not his father's house: "So he set off and went to his father." He will end up where he started, but the fact that he makes the return journey shows that he has come to some insight about himself: he now sees differently. T.S. Eliot has captured the dynamic of the circuitous journey in "Little Gidding" (*Four Quartets*):

> We shall not cease from exploration
> And the end of all our exploring
> Will be to arrive where we started
> And know the place for the first time.

The father's welcome

The father takes the initiative by going to meet his son, even though he is "still far off". The text implies that the father was on the lookout, that he had not given up the stubborn habit of hoping that his son would return. No doubt his eyes often

140

strayed to the road his son had taken when he left home. On seeing his younger son the father does not wait at the house, ready to demand an explanation for his son's wayward behaviour, but is filled with compassion and runs to meet his lost son. The father's compassion is not based on his son's confession; he is compassionate because that is the kind of man he is, and it is his solicitude that will save the younger son. That benevolent movement towards the lost one is particularly important when we remember Luke's context for telling the parable – how the Pharisees and scribes complain that Jesus welcomes sinners and eats with them (Lk 15:2).

There is an interesting rabbinic parallel that makes evident a father's intention of shortening his son's journey of return:[16]

> A king had a son who had gone astray from his father a journey of a hundred days. His friends said to him: "Return to your father." He said, "I cannot." Then his father sent to say, "Return as far as you can, and I will come to you the rest of the way." So God says, "Return to me, and I will return to you."

The father in the parable forgets about his personal dignity and social propriety and runs in public to meet his son. This would have attracted the notice of the villagers, who would soon gather for the street theatre, to see how father and shamed son would confront one another. The father meets his son outside the village; he encloses the lost one in an embrace, kissing him again and again in public. The kiss is not just a gesture of welcome but a sign of forgiveness, as when David kissed his son Absalom when he came into his presence after two years (2 Sam 14:33).

H. Nouwen comments on the abject state of the returned son: "The young man held and blessed by the father is a poor, a very poor, man. He left home with much pride and money, determined to live his own life far away from his father and the community. He returns with nothing: his money, his health, his honour, his self-respect, his reputation . . . everything has been squandered."[17]

Everything the father does is a clear signal of reconciliation to those who are watching. The forgiveness of the father is offered without condition, without waiting for his son's confession of guilt. It is interesting to note that the father does not speak to his son: there is no private conversation between father and son at this point; rather, the father uses the language of his body to communicate his love and acceptance. What the father is doing is not only welcoming his son but also protecting him from the angry disapproval of the villagers. Thus the hired servants and the villagers can interpret the father's body language, without ambiguity, as a public demonstration of forgiveness.

After the father's demonstrative and loving welcome, the younger son begins his prepared speech of contrition: "Father, I have sinned against heaven and before you; I am no longer worthy to be called your son." Missing from his speech is his original proposal for his own survival, "Treat me like one of your hired hands." He had planned to earn his father's approval as a hired servant with his dedication to work; now he realises that his father has given him back his sonship freely. In his father's welcome the younger son realises that he cannot restore the broken relationship between himself and his father; rather, that broken relationship is healed by his father's love. *In the absence of his father the younger son looked for something he could earn with labour; in the presence of his father he is confronted with something given freely and with joy.* As D. Via comments: "In fact repentance finally turns out to be the capacity to forego pride and accept graciousness."[18]

All that the younger son dared hope for on his return was to be treated like a hired servant; now he is publicly welcomed as a guest of honour. In addressing the watching slaves the father continues making his own ceremony of restoring his son publicly to the family and the community. The slaves are told how to treat the returning son, with honour and respect. The son is vested in the best robe (literally, "the first robe"), as if he were a prince being invested at a coronation ritual. The ring, probably a signet ring, is placed on his finger as a sign of status. The robe and the ring are reminiscent of the story of Pharaoh and Joseph: "Removing his signet ring from his hand, Pharaoh put it on Joseph's hand; he arranged him in garments of fine linen, and put a gold chain around his neck" (Gen 41:42). When the slaves are told to put sandals on the feet of the younger son, they are effectively commanded to recognise him as superior to them, for he is a freeman. The son is being publicly restored to his position within the hierarchy of the household.

We remember that all three members of the family have offended the village community by actions that have flouted custom and tradition; thus this family must declare anew its respect and solidarity with the village. The killing of the fatted calf – rather than a sheep or a goat – is an indication that the village would be invited to join in the feast. As K.E. Bailey observes: "To kill a calf and not invite the community would be an insult to the community and a waste for the family. Indeed, the main point of killing such a large animal is to be able to invite the entire community. As with the woman and the shepherd, the joy must be shared on all sides."[19] The invitation is a risk, since the villagers may refuse to attend the homecoming and be reconciled with the family.

The father concludes his speech by offering a reason for eating and celebrating together, "for this son of mine was dead and is alive again; he was lost and is found". In going off to live independently in an alien land, the son was dead to his family, dead to the village, dead to his religious tradition. He lived disconnected from all three traditional ties. Now, thanks to the father's loving welcome and forgiveness, he is going to be reconnected to all three. At the end of his stay in a far country the younger son was also disconnected from food: "no one gave him anything". Now this celebration will reconnect him not only with food but also with feasting in community. The final words of the father's speech – "lost" and "found" – are the catchwords that unite this parable to the preceding two, The Lost Sheep and The Lost Coin.

The father's risk of rejection by the village community pays off handsomely: "And they began to celebrate." The family and the community are now joined together in celebrating the homecoming of the lost son, all of them except the elder brother.

The elder son's response

The younger son has come from a far country, has been met by his father and has been welcomed home to a feast. The elder son now comes in from the fields, remains outside the house and outside the feast, and is met by his father who pleads with him to come home and join the merrymaking. The elder now replaces the younger as the lost son: he is lost not in an alien land but in the wilderness of his own resentment, lost to his family and lost to the village community, who are now united together in celebration.

As the elder son now moves to centre-stage in the drama, a puzzle appears: how can he be ignorant of his brother's return and his father's decision to welcome him by a feast? The setting is clearly contrived, as E. Linneman notes: "The listener to a parable is quite content with such 'stage-productions' as long as it passes only the bounds of probability and not of possibility. If the story as a whole seems credible, he will not be worried by small divergences from what is customary in real life."[20]

In the stage-managed story of the elder son's approach to the house, he hears the sounds of music and dancing; rather than quicken his pace to become part of the celebrations, he calls a young boy (*paides*) to explain the sounds of carnival. The young boy summarises the recent encounter between the father and his younger son: "Your brother has come, and your father has killed the fatted calf, because he has got him back safe and sound." The explanation shifts from the perspective of "son" to that of "brother" – thus emphasising the primary relationship between the two brothers who have yet to meet. The elder brother is angry and refuses to join in the festivity.

The contrast at this point in the story is not between the two brothers but between the elder brother outside the feast and the villagers taking part in the feast. The elder son's refusal to go in publicly humiliates his father and frustrates the latter's attempt to reconcile the family with the village. The music and dancing indicate that the villagers have started to arrive; the process of reconciliation is under way. The elder son's wilful absence makes the rivalry *within the family* a public issue precisely at the time when the feast is aimed at easing tensions *within the village*. The elder son's noted absence will be interpreted as a reproach to the villagers who are attending the feast.

For a second time that day the father comes out to meet a son, hoping that his reconciling presence will lead his son home. Instead of ordering his elder son home or rebuking him for the public insult, the father pleads with him, trying to convince him to do what the rest of the village has managed to do so readily – join in the celebration of welcome. Rather than responding to his father's entreaties, the elder son demands that his father pay attention to his grievances: "Listen! For all these years I have been working like a slave for you, and I have never disobeyed your command; yet you have never given me even a young goat so that I might celebrate with my friends. But when this son of yours came back, who has devoured your property with prostitutes, you killed the fatted calf for him!"

The elder brother describes his life as one based on careful obedience, a predictable life that has been lived following the commands of his father. His dutiful and hardworking way of living, however, has not led him to a sense of worth about himself: his work has become bondage, his sense of self is reduced

144

to that of being a slave. He has never known the excitement of leaving home, the tragedy of downfall in an alien land, the risk of returning home. He has lived his life within the controlled boundaries of working on the farm and being submissive to his father's will; but neither his dedication nor his compliance has led to maturity. He still looks to his father, not himself, to name the problem and the solution.

Not only does he fail to address his father by title but he also disowns his younger brother with contempt – referring to him as "this son of yours" – an avoidance that is met by the father's gentle correction, "this brother of yours". He believes that he has never received due recognition of his dedication, that he has been overlooked and rejected in favour of his undeserving brother. He registers the complaint that his father has never given him even a young goat to celebrate with his friends, revealing his wish to party *outside* the family circle which has hemmed him into his world of obligation. His anger against the younger is stated clearly: the younger son has been destructive of his father's estate and depraved while he himself has slaved on the estate and is faithful. He accuses his younger brother of spending his inheritance on prostitutes: the elder brother now invents "the truth" that is appropriate to his own anger. His dedication and sacrifice have led him to deep resentment and hard-heartedness: in the words of the poet W.B. Yeats, "Too long a sacrifice can make a stone of the heart."

The father responds to his son's outburst by addressing him as *teknon,* which could be translated as "my dear child". The father does not allow his son's bitter resentment to change his own perspective; rather, he remains steadfastly gracious to both his sons. As he countered his younger son's *self-image as a hired servant* by welcoming him as a son, so he now counters his elder son's *self-image as a slave*. The father calls him a dear child, reminds him that he is his life-companion ("You are always with me") and that he shares everything the father has ("all that is mine is yours"). In effect the father tells his elder son that he has become a slave for something that is already in his keep – his inheritance has not been altered by his father's generosity to the younger son.

Reflection

The father's final appeal to his elder son argues that it is only right to celebrate, because "this brother of yours was dead and has come to life; he was lost and has been found". The final appeal serves to unite this parable with the previous two, all three finding their climax in community rejoicing at the return of the lost one.

Given Luke's context for the parable (Lk 15:1-2), especially the presence of the grumbling Pharisees and scribes, it is clear how the drama of the parable mirrors both Jesus' pastoral strategy towards sinners and the Pharisees' strategy of separation.

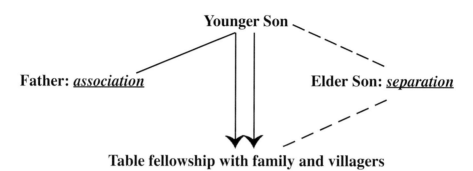

Table fellowship with family and villagers

The father's gentle treatment of his elder son, recognising his legal entitlement to everything the father has while still appealing for reconciliation through table fellowship, is a temperate but firm appeal to the Pharisees to treat sinners with kindness. The father's love is extended not only to the younger son but also to the uncomprehending elder son; he reaches out to both of them, journeys to meet both of them, and tries to get both of them into shared fellowship. His second journey expresses his dream that *together* he and his elder son will move into table fellowship with the younger brother and the villagers. The father challenges his elder son to change his stance from separation to association.

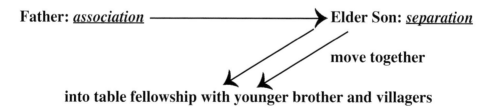

The dynamic of the parable mirrors Jesus' teaching in the parable of The Great Feast, where the challenge is to *feast together,* and where the dominating image is one of the good and the bad alike sharing table fellowship. The unfinished nature of the parable of The Father and Two Sons leaves the Pharisees/readers the opportunity of making their own response to the question: will the elder brother come in from the cold and join the others at the feast? Whatever the answer to that question, Jesus' *own* response has already been demonstrated in his ministry of associating with the lost and sharing table fellowship with them.

[1] See J.R. Donahue, "Tax Collectors and Sinners" in *Catholic Biblical Quarterly* 33 (1971) pp.39-63; "Tax Collector" in *Anchor Bible Dictionary* Vol 6, pp.337-338

[2] J. Jeremias, *The Parables of Jesus,* p.132

[3] T.W. Manson, *The Sayings of Jesus,* p.282

[4] See G. Quispel, "Gospel of Thomas Revisited" in B. Barc (Ed.), *Colloque international sur les textes de Nag Hammadi* (Quebec: Presses de l'Univesité, 1981) p.233

[5] J.D. Derrett, "Law in the New Testament: The Parable of the Prodigal Son" in *New Testament Studies* 14 (1967) p.66 n.1

[6] B.B. Scott, *Hear Then the Parable,* p.415

[7] N. Levison, *The Parables: Their Background and Local Setting* (Edinburgh: T & T Clark, 1926) p.152

[8] G. Bornkamm, *Jesus of Nazareth* (New York: Harper, 1963) p.82

[9] B. Witherington, *Women in the Ministry of Jesus* (Cambridge: Cambridge University Press, 1994) p.38

[10] J. Jeremias, *The Parables of Jesus,* pp.134-135

[11] R. Rohrbaugh, "A Dysfunctional Family and its Neighbours" in V. Shillington (Ed.), *Jesus and his Parables* (Edinburgh: T & T Clark, 1997) p.145

[12] M. Diaz, "Introduction: Economic Relations in Peasant Society" in J. Potter, M. Diaz & G. Foster (Eds.), *Peasant Society: A Reader* (Boston: Little, Brown & Company, 1967) p.50

[13] C. Wright, "Family" in *Anchor Bible Dictionary* Vol 2, pp.763-764

[14] K.E. Bailey, *Poet and Peasant* (Michigan: Eerdmans, 1976) pp.161-162

[15] G. Foster, "Introduction: What is a Peasant?" in *Peasant Society: A Reader,* p.10

[16] Quoted in C. Montefiore & A Loewe, *A Rabbinic Anthology* (London: Macmillan, 1938) p.321

[17] H. Nouwen, *The Return of the Prodigal Son* (London: DLT, 1992) p.41

[18] D. Via, *The Parables,* p.171

[19] K.E. Bailey, *Poet and Peasant* (Grand Rapids: Eerdmans, 1976) p.186

[20] E. Linneman, *Jesus of the Parables,* p.10

Introduction

The parable of The Good Samaritan is one of the most complex and challenging stories in the Gospels, where Jesus takes his own people's favourite enemy – the Samaritans – and turns one of them into a teacher and moral hero. In the parable Jesus challenges his hearers to think again about those whose personal or social identities they deeply despise, those people who are rejected not because of their individual characteristics, compulsions or obsessions but because of institutionalised prejudice against them.

We all have a range of personal and social identities. We are formed from a variety of influences that shape the way we think and act and feel. These controls or influences are not limited to our personal experience, but operate as part of our normal social upbringing. Many of these identities were given to us, many are inherited, and some we make ourselves. Among the ways we define ourselves and other people are:

our gender: male/female	our sexuality
our family	our tribe/clan/region
our country/nationality	our class
our race	our colour
our religion	our politics
our education	our vocation/occupation
our age	our body/health

Some of these identities are more significant than others because they have played an influential role in shaping the way we now are. The important identities will differ from person to person and also from time to time in our lives. We may drop old identities that no longer represent who we are, or we may claim new ones.

For most of us the key identities represent areas in our lives where we have found satisfaction or fulfilment; they also represent areas where we have experienced hurt or oppression. As the psychologist S. Ruth notes:

> It is also a case that we bring our identities into our relationships
> and our leadership. As part of these identities we have internalised

a variety of painful emotions and rigid, inflexible ways of thinking and acting that can interfere with our ability to build effective relationships with others. This is our *internalised oppression*. We bring prejudices, guilt, doubts, misinformation, unresolved conflicts and unhealed hurts that make it difficult to think clearly about ourselves and other people.[1]

Some people are afraid to claim their identity because they fear they will be victimised as a result. Some individuals, tired of being victimised, start to form groups where they can begin the process of claiming their identity, share their stories of hurt, and begin to assert their own rights: thus there are women's groups, gay groups, minority ethnic groups etc. The purpose of these groups is to allow individuals a sympathetic forum to heal the hurts associated with having a particular identity that has met with aggressive disapproval and active mistreatment.

People's social identities are often caught from the surrounding culture. As B.B. Scott observes: "All cultures, modern and ancient draw boundaries between themselves and others, whether it is a matter of defending their turf or building iron curtains. Greeks called everyone who did not speak Greek a barbarian, and Jews divided the world between themselves and Gentiles . . . The appealing and frightening aspect of the parable From Jerusalem to Jericho (Luke 10:30-35) is the recognition that on this journey from Jerusalem to Jericho the recurring effort of humans to divide themselves from others is severely challenged and called into question."[2] Excluding the robbers, each of the five characters in the parable is defined by a distinguishing identity: the victim, the priest, the Levite, the Samaritan, and the innkeeper.

One of the ways we divide ourselves from others is through prejudice, which is often so integral to our way of looking at others that it goes unnoticed. Each of us inherits a mixed bag of beliefs and suspicions; some we have thrown away, others we have made our own. The prejudices that serve to support our sense of superiority are particularly difficult to break down. We can all decorate our insecurity by regarding as inferior those who are different from us, for reasons of race, religion, class, etc. But if our sense of worth is maintained at the expense of other people's dignity, what worth is it?

Being part of a particular group, social or religious or political, can enlarge our world, heighten our sense of belonging and help us form our own identity. It can help us feel good about ourselves as we move within a secure network of relationships.

One of the principal ways any group defines its identity is by asserting its difference from other groups. That pride in difference shows itself in flags and badges, beliefs and attitudes, rituals and traditions. Whatever the nature of the group – a tribe, a religion, a nationality, a political party – loyalty within the group can foster the growth of its members. Sometimes, however, the price for intense loyalty is hostility to outsiders, to those who do not belong to the group.

The real danger comes when members of one group believe that their differences give them the right to lord it over others not belonging to the group. That usually spells violence. This situation is dramatically explored in Shakespeare's *The Merchant of Venice*, when Shylock, a rich Jew, asks why the Christian merchant Antonio can mock him and scorn his nation:

> He hath disgraced me and hindered me half a million; laughed at my losses, mocked at my gains, scorned my nation, thwarted my bargains, cooled my friends, heated mine enemies. And what's his reason? I am a Jew. Hath not a Jew eyes? Hath not a Jew hands, organs, dimensions, senses, affections, passions, fed with the same food, hurt with the same weapons, subject to the same diseases, healed by the same means, warmed and cooled by the same winter and summer as a Christian is? If you prick us, do we not bleed? If you tickle us, do we not laugh? If you poison us, do we not die? And if you wrong us, shall we not revenge? If we are like you in the rest, we will resemble you in that.
>
> (Act III, Scene iii)

Shylock appeals to the basic humanity shared by Jews and Christians alike, one that is easily lost when the differences between the two groups are highlighted. The differences between Jews and Samaritans at the time of Jesus were reckoned considerable by both groups, even though they shared a common origin in the twelve tribes of Israel. The bitterness between the two people becomes the challenge of the parable of The Good Samaritan.

151

The socio-religious background of the parable: Jews and Samaritans

Near the end of the eleventh century BC the Israelite tribes united under David as their king and formed the small national state of all Israel. To consolidate his position David's first act was to take Jerusalem, which had remained a Jebusite enclave between the territories of Judah and Benjamin. Since Jerusalem was not under the control of any tribe, David's choice appeared not to favour any of the tribes in the new coalition. In David's bringing the Ark of the Covenant to Jerusalem (2 Sam 6:17), Jerusalem became the new religious centre of Israel.

Solomon was clearly the beneficiary of David's foreign policy and military victories, allowing him to secure the unity of the kingdom with commercial success. Solomon enlarged the city of Jerusalem and as part of his palace on the north side of the city he began the building of the Temple. His building programmes became so ambitious and costly that he overtaxed the people and introduced forced labour – policies that were to contribute to the undermining of his kingdom following his death.[3] Jeroboam became the leader of those Israelites who opposed Solomon's rule.

The belief that God had chosen David and his descendants to rule Israel for ever (2 Sam 7) carried insufficient weight to suppress the large faction that opposed Solomon. When Solomon's son, Rehoboam, inherited his father's throne, he went to meet representatives of the tribes and clans who lived in the hill country north of Jerusalem. They brought their grievances to the new king and asked him to modify his father's twin burdens of taxation and forced labour. When Rehoboam refused, the assembly at Shechem rejected him (1 Kgs 12:16) and the Davidic dynasty. They offered the kingship to Jeroboam, who established a new state with its capital at Shechem. The northern kingdom was known as Israel, centred on the hill country north of Jerusalem, but also including regions of Gilead and Galilee. The southern kingdom was known as Judah and included the southern hill country and the Negeb.

Though the two kingdoms were religiously, ethnically and culturally parts of the one whole, they were politically independent. The northern kingdom, Israel, was more powerful: it had more natural resources, a larger population, and a greater military capability. The southern kingdom, Judah, was smaller and more centralised, with Jerusalem and its Temple as the focus of national and religious life. Unlike Israel, the kingdom of Judah retained a single dynasty throughout its existence. The two kingdoms existed alongside each other for about two hundred years.

By 732 BC Assyria had reduced Israel to a rump state, ruled by Hoshea. In 724 BC Hoshea began negotiations with Egypt, hoping to secure their support in a revolt against Assyria. When the Assyrians heard about this they attacked Israel's army, and after a three-year siege destroyed Samaria (2 Kgs 17:5). By 721 BC the kingdom of Israel ceased to exist as an independent political state. Although the Assyrians deported a number of the population, most of the people of Israel remained in their land. The Assyrians absorbed the remnant of the Israelite army into their own and repopulated the territory with their own settlers. The new settlers intermarried with the local population, giving birth to a new people known as the Samaritans (2 Kgs 17:24-41). *The Jews of the postexilic period refused to recognise the Samaritans as legitimate Israelites because of their intermarriage with the foreign settlers and acceptance of their ways.*

Although the southern kingdom, Judah, enjoyed a nominal independence, it was a compliant vassal first of Assyria, then of Egypt, and finally of Babylon from 598 to 587 BC. In 587 BC the Babylonians, under Nebuchadnezzar, entered Jerusalem, destroyed the Temple and the palace, and razed a large part of the city. They executed various representatives of Judahite society and led the rest of Judah's leaders into exile in Babylon (2 Kgs 25:8-21). As M. Noth notes: "The book of Ezekiel was edited in Babylonia from the standpoint of conditions there; and so it is a source of information on the mode of life of the exiles. It shows very clearly that the exiles were not 'prisoners' but represented a compulsorily transplanted subject population who were able to move about freely in their daily life, but were presumably compelled to render compulsory labour service. The exiles had villages where they 'dwelt' (Ez 3:15); they were able to build houses and plant gardens there and enjoy their produce. They were able to marry and give in marriage (Jer 29:5)."[4] They retained their ethnic and religious distinctiveness, all the time yearning for Jerusalem which remained the focus of their identity (Ps 137:4-6).

With the return of the exiles in 537 BC there was the growth of Judaism. S. Fraade is surely right when he observes: "While the idea of 'Judaism' as denoting the way of life of the Jewish people or a portion thereof is *traditionally* traced back to the revelation of the Torah to the Israelites at Mt. Sinai in the time of Moses, historically it can be traced back only to the period following the return from the Babylonian Exile in 538 B.C. . . the Greek term *ioudaioi* for Jews (rather than simply Judeans) is first attested in inscriptions from the 3d century BC."[5]

The two main tribes that returned were the larger tribe of Judah and the smaller one of Benjamin, which was eventually absorbed into Judah. A Jew, therefore, was a member of the tribe of Judah.

The first task of the returned exiles was to rebuild the Temple. As Ezra writes: "The heads of the families of Judah and Benjamin, and the priests and the Levites – everyone whose spirit God had stirred – got ready to go up and rebuild the house of the Lord in Jerusalem" (Ezra 1:5). According to Ezra 4:4-5 the Samaritans offer help in the rebuilding but are refused, and they oppose the rebuilding of the Temple and the walls of the city. Not only are the Samaritans rejected but also "the people of the land" (Ezra 4:4) – the people who had remained in Judah during the exile and who had submitted themselves to the Samaria-based regime. The returning exiles were anxious to preserve their own religious independence uncontaminated from what they regarded as unclean and imperfect – in other words they had developed, however understandably, their own ghetto mentality.

The Samaritans claimed Shechem and the adjacent Mount Gerizim as their historic religious and cultural centre. They believed they were the descendants of the tribes of Ephraim, Manasseh and Levi, and that they represented faithful worship of Yahweh from the time the Israelites conquered Canaan. They established a rival priesthood and Temple, which was built around the time of Alexander the Great,[6] and destroyed by the Jewish leader John Hyrcanus around 128 BC. The Samaritans were clearly Temple-oriented and centred. After the destruction of their Temple on Gerizim, they composed the Samaritan Pentateuch, which promoted their claim that they were the true carriers of faith in Yahweh; its ideology emphasises Shechem and Gerizim and downplays Jerusalem and Zion.

By 200 BC the ancient animosity between Jews and Samaritans is reflected in the writings of Ben Sirach:

> Two nations my soul detests,
> and the third is not even a people:
> Those who live in Seir, and the Philistines,
> and the foolish people that live in Shechem.
>
> (Sir 50:25-26)

By New Testament times, the animosity between Jews and Samaritans was commonplace, but not uncontested, as we shall see in the parable of The Good

Samaritan. John 4:9 simply states that the Jews had no dealings with the Samaritans. Jesus instructs the Twelve not to enter any town of the Samaritans, but rather to go only to the lost sheep of the house of Israel (Mt 10:5-6). In the Gospels of Luke and John, however, Samaritans represent in a new radical way the inclusion of the outsider in the true Israel. J. Bowman argues that John consciously addresses himself to the Samaritans.[7]

Luke includes the story of Jesus' rejection in a Samaritan village as an episode in his journey to Jerusalem (Lk 9:51-56). Implicit in the rejection is the objection the Samaritans take to Jesus' destination in Jerusalem. Yet Jesus' rebuke of James and John for their pastoral suggestion of holocaust as a way to deal with Samaritans leaves the door open for a different response. Samaritans hearing the story would recognise that their antagonism was met by Jesus' forbearance. The story of the ten lepers (Lk 17:11-19) is distinctive because the sole individual who returns to give thanks is a Samaritan. The story has a clear suggestion that those alienated from Jews can respond in gratitude and faith to the person of Jesus. This story prepares the way for Acts 8, where Samaria is one of the first missionary fields for the disciples, reflecting a new open attitude of the early church to the Samaritan people.

Luke 10:25-37 (NRSV)

[25]*Just then a lawyer stood up to test Jesus. "Teacher," he said, "what must I do to inherit eternal life?" [26]He said to him, "What is written in the law? What do you read there?" [27]He answered, "You shall love the Lord your God with all your heart, and with all your soul, and with all your strength, and with all your mind; and your neighbour as yourself." [28]And he said to him, "You have given the right answer; do this, and you will live." [29]But wanting to justify himself, he asked Jesus, "And who is my neighbour?"*

[30]*Jesus replied, "A man was going down from Jerusalem to Jericho, and fell into the hands of robbers, who stripped him, beat him, and went away, leaving him half dead. [31]Now by chance a priest was going down that road; and when he saw him, he passed by on the other side. [32]So likewise a Levite, when he came to the place and saw him, passed by on the other side. [33]But a Samaritan while travelling came near him; and when he saw him, he was moved with pity. [34]He went to him and bandaged his wounds, having poured oil and wine on them. Then he put him on his own animal, brought him to an inn, and took care of him. [35]The*

next day he took out two denarii, gave them to the innkeeper, and said, 'Take care of him; and when I come back, I will repay you whatever more you spend.'

[36] "Which of these three, do you think, was a neighbour to the man who fell into the hands of the robbers?" [37]He said, "The one who showed him mercy." Jesus said to him, "Go and do likewise."

The context of the parable

In its present setting the parable of The Good Samaritan is part of a theological dialogue between Jesus and a lawyer about the question of inheriting eternal life and the question of who my neighbour is. The lawyer's first question in Luke is similar to that regarding the greatest commandment in Mark 12:28-31 and Matthew 22:34-40. A literary comparison of the three texts appears to indicate that a question put to Jesus and leading to the quotation from Deuteronomy 6:5 and Leviticus 19:18 was present in both Mark and Q, the common source material shared by Matthew and Luke. While all three evangelists share a similar context, only Luke has the parable, suggesting that Luke has used his editorial freedom to join the parable to the controversy.

In Mark's story a scribe, seeing that Jesus is answering his questioners well, asks Jesus which commandment is the first. He answers the scribe, who then confirms Jesus' teaching and evokes his praise: "You are not far from the kingdom of God" (Mk 12:34). Luke and Matthew are in agreement that the lawyer's intention is to test Jesus. While Jesus answers the question in both Mark and Matthew, in Luke he counters with his own questions: "What is written in the law? What do you read there?" Luke's format of the whole scene can be outlined in two parallel sections:

	Part 1	*Part 2*
Lawyer's question	Eternal life?	Who is my neighbour?
Jesus' counter-question	What is written?	Who proved neighbour?
Lawyer's answer	Dt 6:4/Lev 19:18	One who showed mercy
Jesus' command	Do this and live	Go and do likewise

The lawyer's first answer merges the *Shema*, the basic Jewish creed that commanded an undivided and full love of God, which the faithful Jew was to recite twice a day, with Leviticus 19:18, which commanded love of neighbour. In

Matthew and Mark this combination is attributed to Jesus, whereas in Luke it comes from the lawyer himself. This may mean either that the combination was already a theological commonplace in rabbinic teaching, one that Jesus endorsed, or that the lawyer knew that Jesus originated it and was simply quoting what he had heard. Either way, Jesus commends the lawyer for his faithful recitation, thereby making this double commandment of love into a norm for Christian discipleship, and then challenges him to translate the answer into action: do what you have said and the fullness of life will be yours.

To justify himself, the lawyer is still hoping there is something he can do to appear righteous before God. As K. Barth comments:

> The lawyer does not know that only by mercy can he live and inherit eternal life. He does not want to live by mercy. He does not even know what it is. He actually lives by something quite different from mercy, by his own intention and ability to present himself as a righteous man before God.[8]

While the meaning of the *Shema* is clear and uncontested in the tradition, the meaning of "neighbour" is not. The context of the quotation from Leviticus *clearly limits the definition of neighbour to one's own people*: "You shall not hate in your heart anyone of your kin; you shall reprove your neighbour, or you will incur guilt yourself. You shall not take vengeance or bear a grudge against any of your people, but you shall love your neighbour as yourself: I am the Lord" (Lev 19:17-18).

The difficulty arises around the construction of the word "neighbour", which is used in a twofold sense by the lawyer and by Jesus. In verses 27 and 29, a neighbour is the object of my attention, someone I should love; in verse 36 a neighbour is the subject of attentiveness, someone who shows mercy to me. For some commentators this shift of definition means that the original question remains unanswered, but as T.W. Manson notes:

> Certainly no definition of "neighbour" emerges from the parable: and for a very good reason. The question is unanswerable, and ought not to be asked. For love does not begin by defining its objects: it discovers them. And failure in the observance of the great commandment comes not from lack of precise information

about the application of it, but from lack of love. The point of the parable is that if a man has love in his heart, it will tell him who his neighbour is; and this is the only possible answer to the lawyer's question.[9]

Manson's point is well made. The lawyer seeks definition, and all definitions by their nature establish limits and determine boundaries with precision – just as Leviticus 19:17-19 itself encloses the understanding of neighbour within the confines of the Jewish people. The lawyer's question supposes that there are neighbours and non-neighbours, and that Jesus should clarify the boundaries between these two separate groups. Where are the limits to be drawn? Elsewhere, in Matthew 5:43-44, Jesus quotes traditional teaching while adding his own: "You have heard that it was said, 'You shall love your neighbour and hate your enemy.' But I say to you, Love your enemies and pray for those who persecute you" (see parallel passage in Lk 6:27-36). Jesus turns conventional teaching on its head because in his understanding love shatters boundaries that are set by prejudice and hate; loving those who love you and limiting your greeting only to your brother and sister, even the tax collectors and Gentiles can manage as much.

The parable that Jesus now tells will show the Jews' favourite enemy, the Samaritan, illustrate this dramatic teaching in his merciful attention to the victim in the ditch. And the lawyer will be challenged to be disloyal to his own religious tradition by accepting this Samaritan, not the Jerusalem Temple functionaries in the priest and the Levite, as the one who is worthy of imitation.

The robbery

The drama of the parable opens with a man travelling down the road from Jerusalem to Jericho, a tortuous winding route of about seventeen miles, which runs through desert and rocky hill country. The road, which Josephus describes as "wild and barren",[10] was a notorious hideout for bandits who preyed on passing travellers and pilgrims. About halfway along the route the Crusaders built a fort, on top of the ancient Byzantine fort of Maledomni, to protect pilgrims travelling to Jerusalem. The ancient Israelite road at this point was called the Red Ascent (Josh 15:7). As J. Murphy-O'Connor notes: "To Byzantine and medieval pilgrims the red colour of the rocks suggested rather the place where the traveller in Jesus' parable was attacked by robbers."[11]

Although the man is unnamed and remains anonymous, a Jewish audience would naturally suppose the hapless victim to be a Jew. The robbers strip him naked, beat him, and finally abandon him, leaving him half-dead. As K.E. Bailey comments: "The traveller is able to identify strangers in two ways. He can talk to the unknown man on the road and identify him from his speech, or, even before that, he can identify him by his manner of dress."[12] With the victim being naked and unconscious there is no way to identify him: he is simply a human being desperately in need of support.

For the telling of the parable, Jesus' implied audience is Jewish and they would naturally identify with the man in the ditch, who has been left bruised, broken and unconscious. The perspective of the parable, as R. Funk notes, is "the view from the ditch".[13] Jesus' audience waits with the victim for the arrival of a compassionate figure who will attend him with mercy. It would be natural for a Jewish audience to suppose that the character who would show compassion would be one of their own people, but that expectation is going to be overturned in a most dramatic way. The view from the ditch and the view from the audience will see the stereotype of the Samaritan, the socio-religious outcast, contradicted to become that of the zealous helper.

It might be worth mentioning at this juncture another story of Good Samaritans that might have influenced Luke; it is from post-exilic Judaism and is told in 2 Chronicles 28:1-15. Ahab, king of the southern kingdom of Judah, has been captured by Syria. The northern kingdom of Israel eagerly joins the punishment of Judah, killing and taking prisoners. The Israelites bring home a considerable number of prisoners; they are met at Samaria by the prophet Oded, who denounces their cruelty. The chief men of Samaria support the prophet by refusing entry to the triumphant Israelite warriors:

> So the warriors left the captives and the booty before the officials and all the assembly. Then those who were mentioned by name got up and took the captives, and with the booty clothed all that were naked among them; they clothed them, gave them sandals, provided them with food and drink, and anointed them; and carrying all the feeble among them on donkeys, they brought them to their kindred at Jericho, the city of palm trees. Then they returned to Samaria.   (2 Chr 28:14-15)

This is a story from Hebrew scripture of Samaritans doing works of mercy for Jews, with explicit mention of clothing the naked, anointing, provision of food and drink, carrying on asses to Jericho: all are present, without exact verbal correspondence, in Luke's story.

The priest and the Levite

The first character to appear at the scene of the robbery is a priest, probably on his way home to Jericho, which was a popular domicile for priests and Levites. He may have been returning from service at the Temple, but the parable is silent about this; it says only that he is on this road "by chance". It is by accident, not by providence or fate, that the priest and the Levite happen to be travelling this road.

When the priest sees the afflicted man in the ditch he decides to pass by on the other side. No reason is offered to explain his decision. Fear is a possible reason: fear that the robbers might still be lying in wait for new victims. Possibly the priest might have thought the man dead and was concerned about ritual purity. According to Leviticus 21:1-3, a priest was forbidden to defile himself by contact with a corpse other than one of his closest relatives: "The Lord said to Moses: Speak to the priests, the sons of Aaron, and say to them: No one shall defile himself for a dead person among his relatives, except for his nearest kin: his mother, his father, his son, his daughter, his brother; likewise, for a virgin sister." B.B. Scott quotes the Mishnah on these verses in Leviticus, where it argues that a neglected corpse has priority over ritual purity,[14] but the Mishnah is an early third-century text, and it is very difficult to argue its insights back to the first century.

The priest might well have been following the advice of Ben Sirach who cautions against going to the help of any stranger:

> If you do good, know to whom you do it,
> and you will be thanked for your good deeds.
> Do good to the devout and you will be repaid –
> if not by them, certainly by the Most High.
> No good comes to one who persists in evil
> or to one who does not give alms.
> Give to the devout,
> but do not go to the help of a sinner.
> Do good to the humble,

but do not give to the ungodly;
hold back their bread, and do not give it to them
for by means of it they might subdue you;
then you will receive twice as much evil
for all the good you have done to them.
For the Most High also hates sinners,
and will inflict punishment on the ungodly.
Give to the one who is good,
but do not help the sinner.   (Sir 12:1-7)

Ben Sirach insists that you should first identify the one in need, ensuring he is devout before going to his aid. If God detests sinners, so the argument goes, who are we to provide them with support? While the priest in the parable clearly has the legal right to pass by the unconscious man, in doing so he shows himself to be intolerant of the more pressing need of a fellow human being for emergency help.

Another official of the Jerusalem Temple, a Levite, happens to be travelling on the same road. The Levite comes closer than the priest, for he comes "to the place" where the man is lying half-dead, perhaps to see if he is a neighbour. He makes the same decision as the priest and carries on his way. Perhaps he knew the priest was travelling ahead of him and thought it well to follow the priest's interpretation of the Law. The Law, however, did not make the same purity demands of a Levite that it did of the priest. As J. Jeremias notes: "The Levite was only required to observe ritual cleanliness in the course of his cultic activities. If the Levite, like the priest in Luke 10:31, was journeying from Jerusalem to Jericho, there would be nothing from preventing him from touching 'a dead body by the road.'"[15] Who knows why he does not offer help? Whatever his reason, he disappears from the story.

The identity of both the priest and the Levite is one that is clearly attached to the Temple, and the negative picture of both characters can be seen as a veiled critique on the Temple system itself. As J. McDonald notes: "The parable of the good Samaritan appears to censure the elevation of cultic over moral duties, and thus to criticise cultic values. In this respect, this parable might be held to recapitulate prophetic criticism of the separation of Temple worship from social justice."[16] This will be made all the more telling when the Samaritan produces two sacrificial elements in the Temple's worship, oil and wine, and pours them not as part of a liturgical ritual but as part of a merciful act towards the broken body of a fellow human being.

The Samaritan

When you listen to a joke about an Englishman, an Irishman, and a Scotsman, it comes as no surprise that when you hear the first two identities announced, the third in the *dramatis personae* arrives predictably. That storytelling device of three stock characters, with the joke always on the third, is standard in popular tales. It would confuse the hearer if the joke were announced to be the story of an Englishman, an Irishman, and a Malaysian: the dissimilarity of the third character would upset the habitual expectation of the listener. In this parable the Jewish hearer would naturally expect the triad of a priest, a Levite, and an Israelite. The fact that a Samaritan appears as the third character and the focus of the story would come as a jolt to a Jewish audience.

We have already explored the historical origin of the Jewish-Samaritan conflict and why the enmity between the two peoples had become proverbial. That conflict had sharpened in the lifetime of Jesus when around AD 6, at midnight during Passover, some Samaritans had defiled the Temple by throwing dead men's bones around the court.[17] This provided another reason, were one needed, for the Jews to hold the Samaritans in complete contempt.

In contrast to the first two travellers in the parable, the identity of the third is emphasised by the pointed use of "a Samaritan" at the beginning of the sentence. When the Samaritan appears on the scene, the stage becomes floodlit with fullness of detail. The Greek text devotes 46 words to all that happens before the Samaritan's appearance, while it uses 60 words to describe the Samaritan's devoted attention to the victim. The detailed description of the Samaritan's outreach pulls the hearer/reader into this particular drama of mercy. You watch the Samaritan being moved with pity, go to the unconscious man, pour oil and wine on his wounds, and then bandage them with cloth. You see him put the man on his own animal, bring him to an inn and proceed to take care of him. You observe him pay the innkeeper two denarii and hear him command the innkeeper to care for his penniless charge. Finally, you hear the Samaritan promise to come back and to repay the innkeeper any additional amount that might be required.

There is an interesting parallel between the actions of the Samaritan and the saving action of God in Hosea:

It is he who has torn, and he will heal us;
he has struck down, and he will bind us up.
After two days he will revive us;
on the third day he will raise us up,
that we may live before him . . .
He will come to us like the showers,
like the spring rains that water the earth . . .
For I desire steadfast love and not sacrifice,
the knowledge of God rather than burnt offerings . . .
As robbers lie in wait for someone,
so the priests are banded together;
they murder on the road to Shechem,
they commit a monstrous crime.
In the house of Israel I have seen a horrible thing. (Hos 6:1-10)

In Hosea's prophecy it is God who binds up, who revives, who raises up, who comes, who desires steadfast love and not sacrifice. In the parable it is the rejected outsider, the Samaritan, who ministers these verbs to the afflicted one. In contrast to the two Temple functionaries, it is the Samaritan who illustrates steadfast love, not sacrifice, when he uses the sacrificial elements of oil and wine not on the altar but on the body of the injured man. It is the Samaritan who expresses the preference of God in steadfast love.

After administering first aid by the roadside, the Samaritan leads his animal with its anonymous burden to an inn, probably in Jericho, since there are no inns in the desert. He stays at the inn overnight to care for his new charge, and in the morning, when he must continue his journey, ensures the continued guardianship of the victim by paying the innkeeper to care for him. His compassion is not just a fleeting emotion but an acceptance of continuing responsibility. Since the victim has been robbed of his money, indeed he possesses nothing, his patron promises the innkeeper to make good any further cost on his return journey.

The final exchange

The lawyer's original question concerned the object of love: who is my neighbour? Jesus now asks about the subject of love: "Which of these three, do you think, was a neighbour to the man who fell into the hands of the robbers?" Jesus' teaching in the parable has transformed the question. As T.W. Manson argues: "The principle underlying the question is that while mere neighbourhood does not create love, love does create neighbourliness. Supposing, as we may, that the man who fell among thieves was a Jew, he was in fact 'neighbour' in the technical Jewish sense to the Priest and the Levite; and he was not 'neighbour' to the Samaritan. Yet his lawful 'neighbours' were of no use to him in his extremity, and it was a man who was not his lawful 'neighbour' who helped him. Love created neighbourliness."[18]

Without mentioning the Samaritan by name, the lawyer responds to Jesus' question by recognising the neighbour as "The one who showed him mercy." In this understanding neighbour means possessing the human capacity to identify with the one in need and meet his need with mercy. Not only that, the emphasis in the parable is as much on the identity of the doer as it is on the deeds done. It is worth quoting J.D. Crossan on this point:

> Most importantly, if he (Jesus) wanted to inculcate love of enemies, it would have been radical enough to have a Jewish person stop and assist a wounded Samaritan. But when the story is read as one told by a Jewish Jesus to a Jewish audience, and presumably in a Jerusalem setting, this original historical setting demands that the "Samaritan" be intended and heard as the socio-religious outcast he was . . . The literal point of the story challenges the hearer to put together two impossible and contradictory words for the same person: "Samaritan" and "neighbour". The whole thrust of the story demands that one say what cannot be said, what is a contradiction in terms: Good + Samaritan. On the lips of the historical Jesus the story demands that the hearer respond by saying the contradictory, the impossible, the unspeakable.[19]

Given the climate of acute conflict between the Jews and the Samaritans, what seems impossible to say is that the Samaritan proved himself to be a true neighbour, which is the unavoidable conclusion of the parable. Closing the exchange Jesus says, "Go and do likewise." He challenges the Jewish lawyer with a double imperative *to go* and *to do* as the Samaritan has done

In this final exchange Jesus is defying the Jewish lawyer to accept the Samaritan, his favourite enemy, as his moral model and hero, not his own Temple functionaries in the priest and the Levite. Where the Jewish officials have failed, the outsider has succeeded. In this Jesus is not just challenging the lawyer to be merciful; more importantly, he is questioning the entirely negative Jewish attitude to Samaritans that has been taken for granted for hundreds of years, one that has been enshrined in the Law and in the tradition. *Jesus is effectively challenging the Jewish lawyer to be disloyal to his own religious tradition.*

If your religious tradition invites you to despise other people, then you must be disloyal to that tradition. If loving your neighbour means being disloyal to your tradition, then *disloyalty becomes a virtue*. The ultimate loyalty is love.

Reflection

In the parable Jesus offers his Jewish audience the paradoxical image of the enemy as teacher, the outcast as hero, the religious vagabond as saviour. Jesus passes over the Temple functionaries in the story as quickly as they pass by the victim in the ditch, inviting his listeners to make their own judgement, as he will do explicitly in the parable of The Pharisee and the Toll Collector, about the usefulness of Temple piety. It is the Samaritan who represents true piety.

The journalist Clifford Longley catches the scandal of an outcast Samaritan as Jesus' choice and how we often misunderstand that choice, when he writes:

> In tabloid culture, the Good Samaritan has come to symbolise anybody who does anybody else a favour, especially when they need it badly. So someone who gives a pound to a beggar is called a Good Samaritan. Wrong. The Good Samaritan is the beggar.[20]

As a beggar and outsider himself, the Samaritan has a point of ready identification with the casualty in the ditch. Both of them are victims of violence, both of them have been wounded, in different ways both of them have been passed over by the representatives of the Temple. In the parable of The Good Samaritan it is one victim who goes to the help of another victim; it is the overlooked that befriends the overlooked; it is the wounded that restores the wounded.

We know from our own experience the weight of inherited hostility against people who belong to the wrong crowd, an outlook that is often supported by a magical confidence in one's own crowd. We know that to accept some people in their difference is not only an act of love but also an act of defiance against the bigotry that sometimes passes for religion. Jesus tells us that we must be disloyal to those who would educate our hate. If religion needs hate to nurture it, who needs that kind of religion? Jesus comes to challenge our hate and promote our love.

To return to where we began at the beginning of this chapter. So much of our identity is inherited before we form our own self-identity. It takes us time to define who we are, to discover our own freedom and dignity, to allow others theirs, and shrug off the ancient animosities and inherited prejudice that we have collected on the way. The present can become an enclosure of bigotry or it can become a liberating place that leads us to make room for the world of difference and the diversity of people that God has made.

The more insecure we are, the more threatened we are by difference and those who do not share our way of living or acting or believing. When we know who we are, when we come into our own authority and are content with it, it can lead to appreciation and celebration of difference. Nobody is born catholic; we can only become catholic in our appreciation and outreach. And we can all use our own woundedness as a resource for noticing and helping other people in need.

In the end we have to be loyal to the best in ourselves and our beliefs, and that loyalty can sometimes set us against the group. Groups, religious or political or other, can help us form our identity but we cannot go through life taking *all* our direction from groups. There are endless groups who will happily tell us what to think, how to behave, who to love, who to hate, who to associate with, and who to avoid. But in the end we have to make up our own mind and make up our own heart. When people ask us, "What do *you* think? How do *you* feel?" they presuppose that there is a real individual inside who can respond. We are not just an aggregate of group responses.

A lot of groups tried to write Jesus' script, from his own family in Nazareth through his disciples to the chief priests and the scribes. Jesus writes his own script in his strange choices, his values, his criticisms, and his way of life. By the end of his life he is seen to extend the boundaries of love to include all people. The Gospel challenge, as illustrated in the parable of The Good Samaritan, is to extend the boundaries of compassion even to include our traditional enemies as our teachers, and to use our own experience of hurt to notice and help those who are in need. For Jesus, the map of love has no boundaries and no customs' posts; it lies open to those who would walk its ways.

[1] S. Ruth, "Identity" (Unpublished notes, 1995)

[2] B.B. Scott, *Hear Then the Parable*, pp.189-190

[3] See I. Mendelsohn, "On Corvée Labour in Ancient Canaan and Israel" in *Bulletin of the American Schools of Oriental Research* 167 (1962) pp.31-35

[4] M. Noth, *The History of Israel* (London: A & C Black, 1965) p.296

[5] S. Fraade, "Palestinian Judaism" in *The Anchor Bible Dictionary* Vol 3, p.1054

[6] See Josephus, *Antiquities* 11:302 ff.

[7] J. Bowman, "The Fourth Gospel and the Samaritans" in *Bulletin of the John Rylands University Library of Manchester* 40 (1958) pp.298-308

[8] K. Barth, *The Doctrine of the Word of God* Vol 1 Part 2 in *Church Dogmatics* (Edinburgh: T & T Clark,1956) p.417

[9] T.W. Manson, *The Sayings of Jesus*, pp.261-262

[10] Josephus, *Jewish Wars* 4.474

[11] J. Murphy-O'Connor, *The Holy Land* (Oxford: Oxford University Press, 1998) p.398

[12] K.E. Bailey, *Through Peasant Eyes*, p.42

[13] R. Funk, *Parables and Presence: Forms of the New Testament Tradition* (Philadelphia: Fortress Press, 1982) p.32

[14] B.B. Scott, *Hear Then the Parable*, pp.195-196

[15] J. Jeremias, *The Parables of Jesus*, pp.203-204

[16] J. McDonald, "Alien Grace: the Parable of the Good Samaritan" in V. Shillington (Ed.), *Jesus and his Parables*, p.49

[17] Josephus, *Antiquities* 18.30

[18] T.W. Manson, *The Sayings of Jesus*, p.263

[19] J. Crossan, *In Parables*, pp.63-64

[20] C. Longley, "Why the Good Samaritan is Misunderstood" in *The Daily Telegraph*, 8 May, 1998

Introduction

The parable of The Unjust Judge and the parable of The Pharisee and the Toll Collector, which follow one another without interruption, are inserted into an eschatological discourse (Lk 17:20–18:34) that opens with the Pharisees' question about the coming of the kingdom of God. Jesus tells them that the coming of the kingdom will not be attended by signs and omens, so that people can say, "Look, here it is!" or "There it is!" Neither the time of its coming nor the place of its arrival is open to speculation: "For, in fact, the kingdom of God is among you" (Lk 17:21). Jesus' affirmation seems to suggest that the kingdom is already present in his person and in his ministry of preaching and healing, making the kingdom within the reach of those who are his contemporaries.

Jesus now turns his attention to the disciples, teaching them about the day when the Son of Man will be revealed (Lk 17:22-37). Because the arrival of this day is unpredictable, the disciples will be tempted to believe those who claim to witness signs of it. But if there are going to be no signs, there can be no accurate reading: there is nothing for anyone to interpret. When it does happen – as when lightning flashes in the sky – it will be sudden and clear to all. Comparing the day of the Son of Man with the days of Noah and Lot, there is a warning against a patronising indifference to what is really important in life. When that day comes, there will be an abrupt separation between those who are ready and those who are not, even though they occupy the same bed or grind at the same mill.

If the disciples have been unsuccessful in establishing when all this will happen, they try to discover from Jesus where it will take place. The enigmatic answer comes: "Where the corpse is, there the vultures will gather" (Lk 17:37). Just as the exact location of carrion is clear to the onlooker from the hovering presence of vultures, so, presumably, the presence of the Son of Man will be evident for all to see.

Given the delay in the parousia, Luke offers Jesus' message as a counter to the widespread complacency and indifference of those whose attention is entirely engaged by the ordinary business of "eating and drinking, buying and selling, planting and building" (Lk 17:28). As T.W. Manson comments: "The Christian message is not for those who think that they deserve a better fate than their neighbours, but for those who . . . realise the desperateness of their situation, and ask, 'What must I do to be saved?'"[1] The immediate answer Jesus offers the disciples is "a parable about their need to pray always and not to lose heart" (Lk 18:1). That parable of The Unjust Judge is followed by the parable of The Pharisee and the Toll Collector, which also has something to say about prayer.

For Luke, the most important eschatological attitude of the Christian is prayerful perseverance in the face of difficulty. As the first parable will emphasise stubborn perseverance in making petition, even to a callous judge, the second will deal explicitly with the right kind of prayerful attitude before God, a humble heart, which alone justifies a person before God.

Luke 18:1-8 (NRSV)

[1]*Then Jesus told them a parable about their need to pray always and not to lose heart.* [2]*He said, "In a certain city there was a judge who neither feared God nor had respect for people.* [3]*In that city there was a widow who kept coming to him and saying, 'Grant me justice against my opponent.'* [4]*For a while he refused; but later he said to himself, 'Though I have no fear of God and no respect for anyone,* [5]*yet because this widow keeps bothering me, I will grant her justice, so that she may not wear me out by continually coming.'"* [6]*And the Lord said, "Listen to what the unjust judge says.* [7]*And will not God grant justice to his chosen ones who cry to him day and night? Will he delay long in helping them?* [8]*I tell you, he will quickly grant justice to them. And yet, when the Son of Man comes, will he find faith on earth?"*

The close parallel between the above parable and the parable of The Insistent Neighbour (Lk 11:5-13) has often been noted, as both deal with Jesus' teaching on prayer and perseverance. Because of the obvious similarities in their theme, I have chosen to consider only the parable of The Unjust Judge here. The introduction to the parable in 18:1 is clearly Luke's own construction, relating it to the previous discussion of the day of the Son of Man. Similarly, the ending in 18:8b corresponds to this setting, asking if the Son of Man will find faith when he comes – namely, will he find the disciples continually praying? Perhaps H. Hendrickx is correct when he writes: "The structure of the question seems to suggest that at his coming the Son of Man will find little faith, that many will have lost heart."[2]

With regard to verses 6-8, opinion is divided among scholars between those who see these verses as Jesus' own interpretation and those who read them as the interpretation of the early church. With Rudolf Bultmann,[3] many scholars have regarded the opening phrase of verse 6, "And the Lord said," as an attachment formula providing a transition from the parable to the sayings in verses 7-8. Probably these sayings were originally independent of the parable and have been placed here to distinguish the ready concern of God – "he will quickly grant justice to them" – from the habitual neglect of the recalcitrant judge. These sayings function as a necessary correction, otherwise the reader might be left within the parable, surmising that the unjust judge's callous manner provides an uncritical example of God's way of dealing with petitioners, which would hardly inspire the disciples' belief that they were praying to an attentive God.

Before looking at the parable itself, it might be worth noting here a passage from Ben Sirach that contains so much of the drama and the theology of the parable of The Unjust Judge that it appears to be a source for Luke's writing:

> He (the Lord) will not ignore the supplication of the orphan,
>   or the widow when she pours out her complaint.
> Do not the tears of the widow run down her cheek
>   as she cries out against the one who causes them to fall?
> The one whose service is pleasing to the Lord will be accepted,
>   and his prayer will reach to the clouds.
> The prayer of the humble pierces the clouds,
>   and it will not rest until it reaches its goal;
> It will not desist until the Most High responds
>   and does justice for the righteous, and executes judgement.
> Indeed the Lord will not delay . . .   (Sir 35:17-22)

The power of petition, the wronged but vocal widow, the prayer that reaches its goal, the persistence that is rewarded by God's attention, the eventual dispensation of justice as the petitioner is vindicated: all these are present in Ben Sirach's writing as they are dramatised in Luke's parable. The similarities between the two passages appear too close to be accidental.

The judge

The judge, the principal character in the story, is introduced as a member of the urban elite, a position and social status that would separate him from the majority of the population. Using the model of agrarian societies outlined by G. Lenski (see page 75) the judge would belong to the class of retainers, who were committed to protecting and expanding the rights of the ruling elite. The ruling elite could not ignore the law: gaining control of the law and its interpretation would be essential to securing and maintaining their own position of privilege and power, to transforming the rule of might into the rule of right.

As a judge the protagonist enjoys a high social position, political influence and economic security. In contrast to the widow, who is probably illiterate and has no ready access to political power, the judge is literate and politically well connected. The character of the judge is not calculated to inspire confidence in any petitioner or in any reader. Without an unjust judge, it has to be said, there would be no plot to the story; a just judge would render the widow justice immediately and the parable would have no point to make.

The judge is described as a man "who neither feared God nor had respect for people" – similar to Josephus' description of King Jehoiakim, "neither reverent towards God nor fair towards human beings".[4] This particular descriptive phrase was a popular one, even in extra-biblical literature,[5] and Luke may have used it as proverbial of the judge. Our judge suffers from a double moral affliction that leads one to wonder how he managed to survive as a sitting minister of justice, how he succeeded in keeping his cover story intact of being a judge of the Torah. A judge in Israel was appointed to ensure that God's justice was seen to be done among the people, and fear of God was regarded as a necessary attribute of his office. Thus when King Jehoshaphat sets up judges in the fortified cities of Judah he addresses them:

> Consider what you are doing, for you judge not on behalf of human beings but on the Lord's behalf; he is with you in giving judgement. Now, let the fear of the Lord be upon you; take care what you do, for there is no perversion of justice with the Lord our God, or partiality, or taking of bribes.   (2 Chr 19:6-7)

A judge who is supposed to be judging on God's behalf, but has no fear of God, is clearly a man who refuses to submit to any perspective but his own; he recognises no higher authority than himself. The appeal, "For God's sake, give me justice!" would leave him wholly untouched.

The parable also describes the judge as a man who respects no one. As K.E.

Bailey comments: "The point is that Middle Eastern traditional culture is a shame-pride culture to a significant degree. That is, a particular pattern of social behaviour is encouraged by appeals to shame. The parent does not tell the child, 'That is wrong, Johnny' (with an appeal to an abstract standard of right and wrong) but 'That is shameful, Johnny' (an appeal to that which stimulates feeling of shame or feeling of pride) . . . The problem with the judge is not a failure to 'respect' other people in the sense of respecting someone of learning or high position. Rather it is a case of his inability to sense the evil of his actions in the presence of one who should make him ashamed."[6] The judge cannot be reached by cries of "Shame!" because he is a man whose sense of shame, for whatever reason, has become atrophied within him.

The judge seems unreachable – except, perhaps, by bribery – and isolated in his own independent world. He is resolutely unresponsive to the pleas of the widow. Recognising no influence or authority outside of himself, he has nothing in his life that evokes his allegiance. He remains totally in control and, by his own admission, self-centred. We hear him talking only to himself, complimenting himself that he neither fears God nor has regard for people, and then, unsurprisingly, blaming the victim, the widow, for resisting his refusal to grant her justice. It does not strike him that the widow's persistent demand is a desperate response to his own persistent refusal to grant her justice. His capacity for realistic self-reflection seems, at best, to be negligible. In the end he tells us that he capitulates to her demands because he is worried about his own health. I find it interesting that the appeal that forces the judge to change his mind comes not from God or the widow or other people, but from himself: it is his own protective selfishness, in the end, that makes the widow's case for her.

The widow

The second character is introduced as a widow, a subject that the Law regarded as especially vulnerable and a target of abuse: "You shall not abuse any widow or orphan. If you do abuse them, when they cry out to me, I will surely heed their cry; my wrath will burn, and I will kill you with the sword, and your wives shall become widows and your children orphans" (Ex 22:22-24). The sheer number of passages in the Law and the Prophets that indicate concern for the widow is a measure of how widows were reckoned as objects of exploitation in Israel.[7]

The widow is depicted as a helpless woman and a plaintiff in an unidentified lawsuit. Because the plaintiff is identified as a widow, it would appear that her case concerns her inheritance rights on the death of her husband. S. Safrai has summarised the legal position of widows:[8] a widow enjoys the legal entitlement to be maintained from her husband's estate unless she chooses to return to her father's or brother's house because of kinship patterns; if she does this, she forfeits the right to receive any maintenance from her husband's estate. If she remains unmarried in her deceased husband's house, she will be reduced to a menial role. Whatever she does, there will be pressure on her to remarry, given the disgrace that is often associated with widowhood, a position that is no longer contained within the bounds of the familiar roles of daughter or wife.

With her husband dead, it would appear that the widow is claiming her maintenance from his estate or the amount her husband pledged to her in the event of his death. If her husband did not make a will, defining what amount she was to receive from his estate, the case would require litigation, especially if there were other members of the family making their own claims. As W.R. Herzog notes: "The very fact that her case is in dispute implies that a reasonably large settlement is in dispute, one at least large enough to attract adversaries."[9]

The widow keeps coming to the judge – the imperfect tense expresses the continuity of her action. The parable implies that she has right on her side, that she is trying to secure her due as one who has been wronged; but her legal rights make no impression on the judge who steadfastly denies her justice. Her demand is for justice against her unnamed opponent; she is looking to the judge not to punish her opponent but to vindicate her claim. The widow has no influential family or friends to bring pressure on the judge; the fact that she is representing her own case, without a male family member, is a clear indication of her isolation in the community. She has to rely wholly on her own resources to secure the justice she desperately needs. She is too poor to pay for justice and too ordinary to influence the judicial process: all she has is the justice of her cause and her own persistence.

Neither the adversary nor his case makes any appearance in the parable, perhaps because the judge already represents his case. The parable assumes either that the adversary is influential or that he has paid off the judge with bribes. In delaying the case, the judge is openly at odds with the Law, so the stakes are high enough to induce him to do this. As the judge seems to be representing the case of the widow's adversary, the widow appeals directly to the judge to represent her case by meeting it with justice. There is no higher court of authority that she can appeal to for consideration and correction. She confronts the secret deal between judge and adversary by her open and constant pleading; she breaks in loudly and clearly on the conspiracy of silence surrounding the case. She is wise enough not to denounce the judge in public, which would not serve her cause since he is, by reputation and his own admission, someone who has no regard for others or their opinions. Instead, she demands that the judge be just.

The widow finds a language for her loss and pain; she uses lamentation to express the indignity of being denied injustice. Not surprisingly, the prayer of lamentation forms the largest category of the psalms, and the widow's appeal can be seen within the tradition of biblical lamentation. Lamentations are cries from the heart, groans of anguish, screams for help, protests against what is happening in the midst of life. They are demands shouted from a bed of pain in the hope that God or someone will intervene. The protest at the heart of lamentation tries to free people from remaining mute and isolated in their pain. It aims at change.

Phase 1	Phase 2	Phase 3
mute	*lamenting*	*changing*
speechless	*protesting*	*organising*
powerless	*struggling*	*shaping*

The first step out of speechless isolation is to find a language of protest.[10] This movement refuses to stay with a "humility" that is indistinguishable from pessimism. Pro-active behaviour replaces reactive submission. Lamentation and protest build the bridge between injustice and redress, between powerlessness and change. The purpose of protest is not just self-expression but transformation; the protest is aimed at converting an unjust situation into a just one. This is clearly the purpose of the widow's protest.

By her vocal persistence the widow tests the limits of the judge's endurance. His calculated indifference towards her is met by her purposeful concentration on him. After a period of time he realises that she will not yield but continue to hold tenaciously to her schedule of appearing before him until she receives what she demands. Facing this endless prospect, the judge decides to vindicate her "so that she will not wear me out". The verb *hypōpiazein* literally means to "hit under the eye", an expression borrowed from boxing. The judge fears that her perpetual nagging will wear him out, so to protect his own health he concedes the legality of the widow's claim.

The widow does the judge a favour by exhausting him into justice; he does himself a favour by ridding himself of her in the only way he can – the dispensation of justice. The whole affair has become too painful for this self-regarding judge; thus the compelling reason the judge finds to render justice comes from within himself – it is to secure his own peace.

The final sayings

The sayings that are attached to the parable were in all probability originally independent and added here for the sake of clarification. They clearly function as a conclusion to the parable, one that has to take the form, "how much more will…" if the figure of the judge is not to remain as a figure for God. If an unjust judge eventually concedes to the persistent pleading of a widow for whom he does not care, the argument goes, how much more will God attend the cries of his chosen ones? "Will he delay long in helping them?" (Lk 18:7) is sometimes translated as "even when he delays to help them" (Jerusalem Bible). Our translation makes this a separate question, but in the Greek it is a compound sentence joined to the preceding one that is the real question, namely, "Will not God grant justice to his chosen ones?"

Part of the problem is the meaning of *makrothymein*, which is normally translated "have patience, be longsuffering, forbearing". Clearly the chosen do not want God to delay or to be too longsuffering but to redress what is wrong. T.W. Manson comments on this, using a rabbinical parable:

> A king had two legions of troops. He wondered where he should keep them, and finally decided to have them at a distance from the capital on the ground that if the civilian population became troublesome, and he had to send for the troops, there would be time for the people to come to a more reasonable frame of mind before the troops arrived. So, it is argued, God keeps his wrath at a distance in order to give Israel time to repent. So in this case it may be supposed that the original Aramaic meant "and he postpones his wrath, which he has on their account,"

i.e. he refrains from executing his wrath on those who persecute the elect, thus giving the persecutors time to repent and amend their ways . . . What delays the vindication of the elect is the longsuffering of God towards their foes.[11]

In verse 8 the answer is given, "I tell you he will quickly grant justice to them." This is an assurance that God will indeed listen to the persistent prayers of his chosen ones and offer them redress. It underlines the certainty of God's intervention, one that will happen speedily.

Reflection

In looking back at the parable itself what I find interesting is the Gospel reversal of expectation that a dispassionate judge of the Torah rather than a frantic woman should be offered to the disciples as their teacher. It is not just a social reversal but a gender reversal. The reversal includes its own criticism of a patriarchal judiciary that is manifestly corrupt, one that is formally pledged to give widows special attention. The reversal also sanctions open protest as a means of redressing injustice. The judge's indifference, masquerading as God's purpose, is met by the widow's stubborn objections. She trusts her own instincts over his silence. In this woman the disciples have a new teacher, one who is characterised by the quality of her desperation and her commitment to justice.

Throughout the Gospel of Luke we are introduced to people who become our teachers and, at first sight, they might appear to be eccentric choices to play such an important role on such an important stage. In most religious worlds the conventional teachers are male clerics, whereas the teachers that Jesus presents to us throughout the Gospel narrative seem to be anyone but male clerics; they are ordinary people who tend to be wounded/hurt/outcast, or those who are undergoing or facing crises in their own lives. They are introduced to us as the bearers of Good News, and so many of them appear in the parables. Within the Gospel of Luke we have, for example:

The Gentile centurion whose servant is ill (7:1-10)
The woman who has a bad name (7:36-50)
The demoniac rejected by his own people (8:26-39)
The woman with a haemorrhage (8:43-48)

A little child (9:46-48)
The good Samaritan (10:29-37)
Mary, the sister of Martha (10:38-42)
The man who has to beg for food (11:5-8)
The host who is rejected by his friends (14:16-24)
The shepherd who loses one sheep (15:4-7)
The woman who loses a coin (15:8-10)
The father who loses both his sons (15:11-32)
The steward who is dismissed for being wasteful (16:1-8)
The beggar who dies from neglect (16:19-31)
The Samaritan leper (17:11-19)
The widow who is desperate for justice (18:1-8)
The toll collector who confesses he is a sinner (18:9-14)
The little children (18:15-17)
The blind man of Jericho (18:35-43)
Zacchaeus, a chief toll collector (19:1-10)

When you look at this litany of people, they appear, at first sight, to be an unlikely group of evangelists – few, I imagine, would be invited to a biblical consortium – yet all of them, in spite of their social position or vulnerability, teach us something about the values of Jesus. Perhaps it is better said that we are drawn to them because of their vulnerability rather than in spite of it.

Not least on the list is the desperate widow who takes on the weight of the legal system and, despite the unlikelihood of a positive outcome, refuses to accept the fate assigned to her by her social position or by the obduracy of the judge. She refuses to play the role of the silent, mourning widow who suffers her loss without protest; she refuses to lead her life off-stage, unseen and unacknowledged. Instead, she enters the drama and shamelessly dominates the centre of the stage, effectively stealing the scene from the main character. She stays centre-stage, taking on the world of patriarchal power until she eventually succeeds in winning recognition for who she is: a poor widow who stays hungry for justice until she receives what is her right. We, who watch her, can only applaud such a spirited performance.

In the Christian tradition the widow is our teacher. Her example is particularly vital in a modern world where we have become accustomed to instant coffee and instant delivery and instant results, a world of immediacy where we can become easily impatient with short delays. But the values of Jesus are not instantly available or attainable: values like justice and peace take time to establish and even more to uphold. The danger in our modern world is that we give up too readily, that we rest our case too easily, that we stop groaning for justice too quickly. Perhaps we are not desperate enough . . .

The widow teaches us not to be overawed by the powerful who have the last word, not to give permission to the corrupt to rule our lives. She teaches us to be equal to our desperation by being stubborn in our commitment; she challenges us to invest our time and energy in what we believe to be right, to face up to formidable opposition in the war of nerves, even if we have to batter down social boundaries that would keep us from our objective. She teaches us the art of protest. And she leaves behind her the echo of her cry: "Stay crying for justice until you exhaust the mighty into justice."

[1] T.W. Manson, *The Sayings of Jesus*, p.144

[2] H. Hendrickx, *The Parables of Jesus Then and Now* (Manila: St Paul, 1983) p.321

[3] R. Bultmann, *History of the Synoptic Tradition* (Oxford: Blackwell, 1963) p. 175

[4] Josephus, *Antiquities* 10.5.2

[5] See E. Freed, "The Parable of the Judge and the Widow (Luke 18:1-8)" in *New Testament Studies* (1987) 33 pp.42-43

[6] K.E. Bailey, *Through Peasant Eyes*, p.132

[7] See, for example, Deuteronomy 10:16-18; 14:28-29; 24:17-18; 26:12-13; 27:19; Isaiah 1:16-17, 23; 10:1-2; Jeremiah 7:5-7; 22:3; Ezekiel 22:6-7; Zechariah 7:8-12; Psalms 68:5; 94:6; 146:9

[8] S. Safrai, "Home and Family" in S. Safrai & M. Stern (Eds.), *The Jewish People in the First Century* Vol 2 (Philadelphia: Fortress, 1976) pp. 787-791

[9] W.R. Herzog, *Parables as Subversive Speech*, p.224

[10] See D. Soelle, *Suffering* (Philadelphia: Fortress,1975) pp.61-86

[11] T.W. Manson, *The Sayings of Jesus*, p.308

Luke 18:9-14 (NRSV)

[9]*He also told this parable to some who trusted in themselves that they were righteous and regarded others with contempt:* [10]*"Two men went up to the temple to pray, one a Pharisee and the other a tax collector.* [11]*The Pharisee, standing by himself, was praying thus, 'God, I thank you that I am not like other people: thieves, rogues, adulterers, or even like this tax collector.* [12]*I fast twice a week; I give a tenth of all my income.'* [13]*But the tax collector, standing far off, would not even look up to heaven, but was beating his breast and saying, 'God, be merciful to me, a sinner!'* [14]*I tell you, this man went down to his home justified rather than the other; for all who exalt themselves will be humbled, but all who humble themselves will be exalted."*

Introduction

Luke establishes the framework of this parable by describing the target audience as "some who trusted in themselves that they were righteous and regarded others with contempt". These are the people who have faith in themselves, rather than in the mercy of God, because they are persuaded that their personal moral achievements and obedience to the Law make them blameless, thus securing God's approval. This attitude embraces a contemptuous dismissal of all those who are not like them, those who cannot share their righteous self-satisfaction. That sense of being blameless while dismissing or persecuting others is reflected by Paul when he reminisces about his own Pharisaic attitude: ". . . a Hebrew born of Hebrews; as to the law, a Pharisee; as to zeal, a persecutor of the church; as to righteousness under the law, blameless" (Phil 3:5-6).

Luke's editorial construction inevitably leads the readers of the parable, as opposed to Jesus' listeners, to judge the Pharisee before the parable begins, a judgement that Luke repeats in his editorial conclusion in verse 14b, "for all who exalt themselves will be humbled, but all who humble themselves will be exalted". Verse 14b is best seen as a floating saying (it also appears in Mt 18:4; 23:12 and Lk 14:11) which has been attached to the parable either in the tradition or by Luke himself. (For the setting of this parable in Luke's Gospel and its relation to the parable of The Unjust Judge, see the Introduction in the previous chapter.)

Luke's introduction and conclusion, together with Jesus' final comment in

14a, establish the character of the Pharisee as haughty and self-righteous, someone who habitually scorns other people and whose confidence is grounded in his own moral achievements. While Luke aims the parable at people like the individual Pharisee in the parable, it would be a mistake to dismiss all Pharisees by caricaturing them as haughty and censorious, thus reducing them to stereotyped villains. Certainly, spiritual pride was reckoned a particular moral danger in Pharisaism, as recognised by the great Pharisaic leader, Hillel, who operated in the first century BC. He noted: "Keep not aloof from the congregation and trust not in thyself until the day of thy death, and judge not thy fellow until thou art come to his place."[1] It is only fair to presume that during the time of Jesus' ministry some Pharisees lived out the advice of Hillel.

The parable opens with two men going up to the Temple and concludes with the same two characters – now their order is reversed – leaving the sacred space of the Temple and going down to the ordinary space of their homes. In the parable there are three principal "characters" that appear on the scene: there is the Temple itself, a Pharisee, and a toll collector. The setting of the parable in the sacred precincts is essential to the story, making the Temple an important player in the drama. Among other things the Temple stands for a religious standard that has its own opinion of the other two characters. As H. Mottu notes, the Temple "determines from the outset the rules of the game".[2]

All three characters were well known to Jesus' hearers; all three, as soon as they appeared in the story, would have been greeted by predictable responses from the hearer: the Temple is the sacred place of God's dwelling, the Pharisee is the upright religious man, and the toll collector is the despised outcast. By the end of the parable, however, the hearer is left confused about all three characters, not least because the despised toll collector's prayer is seen as acceptable within the precincts of God's own house while the Pharisee's prayer is not. How can a moral outcast find justification before God within the Temple precincts? What does that say about the Temple and the Pharisee? What does it say about the old order? We shall look at the three characters in turn.

The Temple

No other building in the ancient world has commanded so much attention through the ages as the Temple in Jerusalem. Apart from the seventy years of desolation in the wake of the Babylonian conquest of Jerusalem, the influence of the Temple lasted a millennium: from the origins of the monarchy in the tenth century BC, when it was constructed by King Solomon, until the capture of Jerusalem in AD 70, when Titus and the tenth legion left the whole of the Temple mount in smouldering ruins. During the millennium of its influence the Temple played not only a central religious and cultic role in Israelite life, but it also functioned at a political level, from its origins as a state institution which gave legitimacy to the monarchy until its destruction by the Romans as the focal point of Jewish identity.

The basic term for the Temple was *bêt Yahōeh* or *bêt 'ēlōhîm*, "house of Yahweh" or "house of God" – the word "house" stressing its residential nature as the divine dwelling-place on earth. Although the God of Israel was viewed as a transcendent being, the need for the nearness and protection of the divine power led the people of Israel to establish a place in which access to the transcendent God could be secured. The elaborate and costly furnishings were an indication of the building's occupant, with the glory of those furnishings signifying the Glory within.

The belief in the divine presence in the Temple inevitably involved the notion of purity for those who approached. The Temple building stood within an enclosure known as the Priests' Court. Outside that area was the Court of Israelites. Still farther removed from the central sanctuary was the Women's Court. Finally, the whole Temple area was bounded by a larger Outer Court, to which Gentiles were admitted. Beyond the Temple precincts was profane territory. The idea was a Holy of Holies standing at the centre of a series of concentric rectangles which were arranged according to a decreasing scale of purity as they became farther removed from the holiest place. This symbolism of degrees of purity was repeated in the people who were allowed access to the several courts, from the high priest at one end, who entered the Holy of Holies once a year, to ordinary priests, Levites, lay Israelites, women, and finally Gentiles. As C. Meyer writes:

> This carefully arranged gradation involves a consciousness that the closer one gets to the inner sanctum, the nearer one is to the perfection of the divine presence. Even if an ordinary individual can never approach the holiest place, the existence of the concentric circles, as it were, of increasing holiness signified that the Holiest One of all could be found at the sacred centre. The purity of the sacred centre involved physical cleanliness.

But it also involved the moral perfection associated with the nature of Yahweh. The Psalmist who expressed the need for both "clean hands" and a "pure heart" in order to ascend the Temple mount (Ps 24:3-4) points to the nature of the cosmic centre as moral centre.[3]

The Temple as moral centre is symbolised by the physical presence of the two tablets of stone contained in the ark, on which were written the moral imperatives of the Israelite covenant with God. The Holy of Holies symbolised not only the divine presence of God among his people but also the establishment of social order through the Law. At the heart of the most sacred place in the Temple, which was the most sacred place in Judaism, was the Law.

The Temple is not only the venerable place of worship and the only legitimate sanctuary but also the equivalent of a central bank, including treasures and treasuries that held vast wealth and the capacity to finance many projects. As the Temple was an institution of economic power, it was also one of economic need, a need that was addressed by the collection of tithes and taxes from the Jewish faithful. Thus the Jewish people were faced with two taxations – one exacted by the Roman occupying power and the other by the Temple. In the parable there are two toll collectors – the toll collector who is a minor functionary of the *Roman* taxation system and the Pharisee who is a representative retainer of the *Temple* system.

M. Borg[4] reduces the complicated list of Temple taxes to three major ones:

1) the annual "wave offering" – the offering of first fruits established at between one and three per cent of the produce;
2) the annual ten per cent tithe, which provided financial support for the priests and the Levites;
3) the second tithe, which was dedicated for a variety of religious purposes during the six-year cycle between sabbaticals.

Taxation was an essential part of the devotional life of every Jew. The cost of Temple piety was not only expensive but could be crushing for the huge majority of the agrarian population, which was composed of peasants. Luke will later tell of a poverty-stricken widow who puts all she has to live on into the Temple treasury (Lk 21:1-4). In this passage Jesus decries the ills of official devotion that leaves the poor widow with nothing. As A.G. Wright notes on this passage:

> Jesus' saying is not a penetrating insight on the measuring of gifts;
> it is a lament: "Amen, I tell you, she gave more than all the others."
> Or, as we would say: "One could easily fail to notice it, but there is
> the tragedy of the day – she put in her whole living." She has been
> taught and encouraged by religious leaders to donate as she does,
> and Jesus condemns the value system that motivates her action,
> and he condemns the people who conditioned her to do it.[5]

In this story Jesus deplores the fact that the Temple can effortlessly eat up the livelihood of poor widows. By the time the Temple elite is finished with the pious poor, they are left with nothing. In this scene Jesus is not so much praising the individual widow's generosity as lamenting a system that demands everything from her if she is to be regarded as upright by the institution she supports. Not surprisingly this story is followed by the discourse on the destruction of Jerusalem (Lk 21:5-7). When some people admire the beauty of the Temple's fixtures, it prompts Jesus to speak of the coming destruction of the Temple, when everything will be destroyed. That destruction Jesus has already acted out in his symbolic judgement on the Temple system, a dangerous enactment that prompts the chief priests and the scribes to try to do away with him (Lk 19:45-48).

In the parable the Pharisee is seen as a dedicated and zealous supporter of the Temple and its system: "I give a tenth of all my income." As a generous taxpayer of the Temple, one would expect the Temple, which houses the presence of God, to look with kindness on his prayer. Similarly, one would expect the Temple to look on the toll collector with undisguised disapproval, for he is dedicated to collecting taxes in support of the Roman imperial system; he is a competitor, one committed to supporting another economy. In the parable, however, there is the radical teaching that God does not look at either of them through the medium of the Temple. *God's view is independent of the Temple's view.*

The Pharisee
The Pharisees were one group among many characterised by a distinctive way of living Judaism, a social movement that sought to change society by a stricter Jewish way of life based on adherence to the Law and oral tradition. Since their

social position was not stable like hereditary traditional leaders (priests, village elders, etc.) they had to recruit new members and compete for power with those who already exercised it. Their differences from other Jewish groups, including Jesus and his disciples, were sufficient to provoke conflict and dispute. After reviewing the major sources on the Pharisees, Anthony Saldarini writes:

> A major question unanswered by the sources concerns the daily activities of Pharisees and the source of their livelihood. The older theory that they were urban artisans is very unlikely because artisans were poor, uneducated and uninfluential. The more common theory that the Pharisees were a lay scribal group, a group of religious scholars and intellectuals who displaced the traditional leaders and gained great authority over the community is likewise very unlikely. Though some Pharisees were part of the governing class, most Pharisees were subordinate officials, bureaucrats, judges and educators. They are best understood as retainers who were literate servants of the governing class and had a programme for Jewish society and influence with the people and their patrons. When the opportunity arose, they sought power over society.[6]

The traditions that stem from the early first century mostly refer to the Pharisees' concern for ritual purity, agricultural tithes and sabbath observance. The Pharisaic stress on purity rules created artificial boundaries between themselves and other groups, an activity typical of minorities who want to retain their separate identity. Their purity rules and tithing separated what they considered their dedicated life from everyone and everything they reckoned as ambiguous or abnormal. Thus the Pharisee in the parable not only stands apart from everyone else but also takes pride in his belief that he is not like other people whom he is pleased to register with disapproval.

Both the Pharisee and the toll collector go up to the Temple to pray. The setting is probably the morning or afternoon atoning sacrifice that was offered as part of the daily public worship of the Temple. The setting is similar to the opening scene of Luke's Gospel, where Zechariah the priest is offering incense: "Now at the time of the incense offering, the whole assembly of the people was praying outside" (Lk 1:10). As Luke indicates, the time for personal prayer during corporate worship was when the priest made the incense offering; this was done after a lamb was sacrificed for the sins of Israel. The offering was entirely consumed by fire, no part of the flesh being available for human consumption: it was a complete burnt offering. Thus the two men in the parable make their private prayers, at the appropriate time, during the public service of atonement.

As our translation indicates, the phrase *pros heauton* ("by himself" or "to himself") refers to the Pharisee's standing rather than to his praying. The normal posture for prayer was standing. The Pharisee stands aloof from the other members of the assembly because, no doubt, he does not want to risk contracting uncleanness from brushing against sinners at the very time when he is praying. As a member of the "separated ones" he is obliged to keep his distance from sin and sinners, a moral and physical stance that is utterly essential to his religious identity.

The Jewish tradition was to pray aloud, so the presumption is that the Pharisee prays likewise. Although Western readers automatically dismiss the Pharisee's prayer as self-righteous and haughty, it is more probable that Jesus' hearers would have heard it as the thanksgiving prayer of an upright man who was encouraging fidelity to the Law. It is important, however, that the Pharisee's prayer be accepted at face value if the parable's disturbing conclusion is going to work.

The Pharisee's prayer is not dissimilar to the following two examples, the first from the Talmud and the second from the Qumran literature:

> I thank thee, O Lord, my God, that thou hast given me my lot with those who sit in Beth ha-Midrash (the house of study) and Thou hast not set my portion with those who sit at street corners; for I rise early and they rise early, but I rise early for words of Torah and they rise early for frivolous talk. I labour and they labour, but I labour and receive a reward and they labour and do not receive a reward. I run and they run, but I run towards the age of the life to come and they run towards the pit of destruction. (b. Berakot 28b)

> I praise thee, O Lord, that thou hast not allowed my lot to fall among the worthless community, nor assigned me a part in the circle of the secret ones. (1QH 7:34)

The structure of both prayers is similar to that of the Pharisee. Neither the Talmud nor the Qumran literature offers the prayers as examples of self-absorption or boasting; they are presented as thanksgiving prayers that bless God for good fortune. The Pharisee gives thanks to God that he is not like the rest – people whom the Temple and the Law would certainly place outside their range of approval. His list identifies thieves, rogues, adulterers, and the particular toll collector who is standing within earshot. As V. Shillington observes: "The claim that he was 'not like other people' was likely a source of envy rather than anger. His thanksgiving for not being like other people, a claim which so jars on modern egalitarian ideals, was quite justified. No one would have condemned it. Luke's editorial frame (v.9) implicitly condemns the attitude but this was a later concern when Church and Pharisee were in spiritual competition."[7]

After describing what he is not, the Pharisee continues his self-definition by listing what he does: "I fast twice a week; I give a tenth of all my income." Jews were expected to fast only annually, for the Day of Atonement (Lev 23:27), whereas this Pharisee fasts twice each week, an ascetical practice that would be regarded by ordinary people as admirable and exceptional, and certain evidence of the man's piety. This pious practice was confined to strict Pharisaic circles and was practised on a Monday and Thursday. Fasting was an act of mourning and penitence and, although not stated, it is possible that the Pharisee fasts twice weekly as an act of contrition on behalf of those who are not like himself in their dedication to the upright life.

Tithes were levied on seed, grain, wine, oil, and the firstborn of every herd and flock (Dt 14:22-23), but those who were particularly strict also paid tithes on non-agricultural products, thus exceeding the demands of the Law. Those who did not pay tithes on these products rendered the products unclean and thus became impure in their use of them. To ensure personal purity the Pharisee pays tithes on everything he owns, although it is only right to observe that anyone who can fast twice a week must be well fed, and anyone who can tithe a tenth of his income must be well off compared to the majority of people.

There is no criticism of the Pharisee *inside* the parable, no hint that this man is a hypocrite or that his virtuous life is a theatrical pretence. One thing is certain: the Pharisee is clearly exceptional as a taxpayer in his support of the Temple. Both he, and Jesus' original hearers, would expect that the God of Israel, resident in the Temple, would surely accept his prayers. His prayer, after all, is not being said in the privacy of a home or on the open road; it is being offered in the shadow of the Temple, during public worship, while the priest is offering the incense.

The toll collector

Part of the Pharisee's prayer does appear as a calculated attempt to publicly shame the toll collector, who is clearly out of place in the Temple court and in the presence of the other worshippers. As the Pharisee stands prominently by himself, the toll collector stands "far off" – probably on the margin of the Court of Israelites.

The toll collector is part of a despised trade, one that put him beyond the boundaries of religious and social approval because he was regarded as someone who made a vocation out of dishonesty. In his study of the difference between tax collectors and toll collectors, J.R. Donahue observes:

> One of the chief functions of the prefect of Judea was his role of financial overseer. During the rule of the prefects and procurators the direct taxes, the poll tax and the land tax were not farmed out. The officials in charge of collecting these were in direct employ of the Romans. Though Roman citizenship was not required for the office of tax collector, it was often granted and many of the tax collectors *de facto* were Jews. The tolls and numerous other tariffs were probably at this time auctioned off to the highest bidder, so that *ho telōnēs* is properly a toll collector and not a tax collector.[8]

The toll collectors were responsible for the collection of custom duties at travel points such as Capernaum and Jericho, and they were popularly regarded as thieves because of their habit of charging exorbitant tariffs and making profits for their employers, the toll contractors, from their calculated dishonesty. Working directly with the public, they were the visible face of their invisible masters, the retainers who had won the contracts. The toll collectors themselves probably survived on subsistence-level wages paid by the retainers and could be readily replaced by those who were so desperate for work that they would risk the castigation of their own people.

The fact that toll collectors charged so many anonymous people made it impossible that they would know the identity of their victims, much less make restitution to them according to the Law. It is this group that Jesus is accused of consorting with, even eating with, in the Gospels – an accusation levelled by the

Pharisees and scribes (Lk 5:30; 15:2). N. Perrin goes further and argues that toll collectors were regarded as "Jews who made themselves Gentiles" and that Jesus' regular table fellowship with them was a key reason why the religious authorities in Jerusalem wanted him crucified.[9]

As the Pharisee stands by himself in a space of prominence in the Temple court, the toll collector stands far off, at the edges of the court, in order to be inconspicuous among the praying assembly. He dares not lift up either his eyes or his hands to heaven – uplifted hands were a normal gesture in prayer. With head bowed he starts beating his breast, the seat of the heart, from where all good and evil originate (see Mt 15:19).

In beating his breast the toll collector prays in a manner that speaks of extreme mourning, even despair, a gesture that Luke uses again at the death of Jesus: "And when all the crowds who had gathered there for this spectacle saw what had taken place, they returned home, beating their breasts" (Lk 23:48). These two instances are the only examples in the whole of biblical literature when this gesture of beating the breast is used. Kenneth Bailey comments on the use of the gesture in the Middle East: "Women customarily beat on their chests at funerals, but men do not. For men it is a gesture of *extreme* sorrow and anguish and it is almost never used."[10] The rare use of it in the parable clearly indicates the extremity of the toll collector's mourning for his own life.

His prayer is in the form of a plea, which our translation renders: "God, be merciful to me, a sinner." The phrase Luke uses is not *eleēson me* ("have mercy on me" – see Lk 18:13) but *hilasthēti moi*, which is better translated as "make atonement for me" as it is translated in the only other place the verb is used in the New Testament: "to make a sacrifice of atonement for the sins of the people" (Heb 2:17). The noun *hilastērion* is used in Romans 3:25; Hebrews 9:5; 1 John 2:2; 4:10; in each case the idea of atonement, not mercy, is clearly present. This meaning fits well into the present context of the parable, which is the atonement sacrifice offered by the priest for the sins of the people. While the priest is offering the incense the toll collector longs and prays for the benefit of the atonement sacrifice on his own sinful life.

The toll collector beats his breast and makes his brief plea in prayer. But as T.W. Manson warns: "It is a great mistake to regard the publican as a decent sort of fellow, who knew his own limitations and did not pretend to be better than he was. It is one of the marks of our time that the Pharisee and the publican have changed places; and it is the modern equivalent of the publican who may be heard thanking God that he is not like those canting humbugs, hypocrites, and killjoys, whose chief offence is that they take their religion seriously."[11]

The toll collector says nothing about changing his ways, nothing about repentance. He promises no change, no reparation, and no retribution. Unlike Zacchaeus, the *chief* toll collector in the next chapter (Lk 19:1-10), the toll collector does not pledge to give half his money to the poor and repay fourfold everyone he has defrauded. Had he done that, even the disapproving Pharisee would have endorsed his decision. Although the toll collector expresses discontent with his life, acknowledging a truth that everyone knows – he is a sinner – the man says nothing about abandoning his sinful way of life and is totally silent about his responsibility for his future.

None of Jesus' hearers would have expected the toll collector's prayer to be accepted. It is a prayer that asks for everything and promises nothing, a prayer that looks to God to make atonement for his sins, but takes no responsibility for the subject's own pattern of life. Apart from that, for Jesus' hearers the toll collector was a minor functionary in a corrupt oppressive system, a collector not for the Temple but the ruling elite. He is dedicated to supporting the economy of Roman taxation not the economy of the Temple; his priority is the Roman system not the sacrificial system, a precedence that would have forced ordinary Jews first to pay their dues to Rome rather than pay their tithes to the Temple. It seems unlikely, therefore, that the Temple will look kindly on his prayer.

Reflection

The shock comes with Jesus' comment on the parable: "I tell you, this man went down to his home justified rather than the other." The verdict Jesus pronounces goes counter to what anyone would have anticipated, indeed it would have sounded outrageous to his original listeners. The toll collector, who has consistently disobeyed the Law that is honoured in the holiest place in the Temple, has found favour with God and has been acquitted; the Pharisee, for all his commitment to exceeding the demands of that same Law, has found neither favour nor justice with God. What fault has the Pharisee committed? What reparation has the toll collector made? Jesus' conclusion is unimaginable, bizarre, and subversive. He overturns the expectations of his hearers, leaving them bewildered and puzzled. And the puzzle is not in the parable but in Jesus' comment on it.

Jesus speaks with authority on behalf of God, but *not the God of the Temple who would have confirmed the Pharisee's virtuous life and convicted the toll collector of his sinfulness and way of life.* Whose is the real God: the God of the Temple, who would have found the toll collector guilty as charged by the Pharisee, or the God of Jesus, who finds favour with the outcast? It is as if Jesus throws away the map that guides our belief in how God finds some people good and some bad. As B.B. Scott comments: "The map has been abandoned, it can no longer predict who will be an insider or outsider. The parable subverts the metaphorical structure that sees the kingdom of God as Temple. Given this metaphorical system, things associated with the Temple are holy and in the kingdom, and things not associated with the Temple are unholy and outside the kingdom. In the parable the holy is outside the kingdom and the unholy is inside."[12] Without our familiar map, it is all very confusing . . .

By his comment on the parable Jesus replaces the spirituality of the Temple with his own. This is illustrated most clearly in Mark 11:12-25, where the principal scene is also the Temple.[13] On his way to Jerusalem Jesus curses a fruitless fig tree. On reaching the city he begins a one-man riot in the Temple, expelling merchants and pilgrims alike. He then overturns the money tables and the seats – a clear symbol of destruction. In refusing anyone passage who was carrying anything, it appears that Jesus wants to bring the whole sacrificial system of the Temple to a halt. That the fig tree is seen "withered away to its roots" the next morning is a dramatic image of what will surely befall the whole Temple system. Immediately following this passage, Jesus speaks about the importance of faith and prayer. The connection between prayer and the Temple has now been severed. The power of prayer resides no longer in the Temple but in those who have faith: "So I tell you, whatever you ask for in prayer, believe that you have received it, and it will be yours" (Mk 11:24).

In the parable of The Pharisee and the Toll Collector, together with Jesus' comment on it, there is a similar dynamic in which the Temple and its spirituality are rejected. Against both the values expressed by the Pharisee and the values symbolised by the Temple as the moral centre of Judaism, the toll collector appeals directly to God. Because he has not approached the Temple court either with "clean hands" or "a pure heart" (Ps 24:3-4) he does not challenge the Pharisee's degrading estimation of him; instead, he goes on to appeal directly to the God who atones for all sins. In Jesus' reading God replies positively. As W.R. Herzog asks: "And if toll collectors and sinners are justified in the very precincts of the Temple itself, then how is one to evaluate a Temple priesthood and its scribes who declare that nothing of the kind is possible?"[14] More importantly, how is one to evaluate the Temple itself?

Jesus exposes the old order, represented by the Temple and the Pharisee, and rejects it in favour of the spirituality of a broken spirit. The God Jesus refers to is one who has made an earlier appearance in Psalm 51, one who delights not in the sacrifice of burnt offerings but favours a broken and contrite heart:

> Have mercy on me, O God, according to your steadfast love;
> according to your abundant mercy blot out my transgressions.
> Wash me thoroughly from my iniquity,
> and cleanse me from my sin. . .
>
> For you take no delight in sacrifice;
> if I were to give a burnt offering, you would not be pleased.
> The sacrifice acceptable to God is a broken spirit;
> a broken and contrite heart, O God, you will not despise.
>
> (Ps 51:1-2, 16-17)

Jesus establishes a spirituality that is centred on a crushed spirit before the presence of God. The toll collector is welcomed into God's favour because he adopts this prayerful stance before God; the Pharisee is rejected because he represents only his own pious achievements and his moral disapproval of those who do not share the story of his religious success. In this subversive portrait of religion, God is no longer controlled by religious elites, no longer accessed through the superior ritual of burnt offering, no longer mediated through the approval of priests. He is accessible to all sinners who approach him in honesty and humility.

That accessibility is reflected in Jesus' own table fellowship with toll collectors and sinners. His unrestricted table fellowship mirrors his belief in people's unrestricted access to God. Where the Temple and the synagogue say no to certain categories of people, Jesus says yes in his welcome. He connects with them, associates with them, and eats with them in the fond hope that in this atmosphere of acceptance they will change their minds about how they lead their lives.

In being accessible to them, he will provoke the aggressive disapproval of religious leaders; in the end he will face the penalty for his strange choices in a violent execution. The new world that Jesus opens up in his parables is a world that threatens too many people whose investment is in the old order of things. Jesus pays the ultimate price for exposing the old order.

[1] Hillel, *Aboth* 2:5 quoted in H. Danby (Ed.), *The Mishnah* (Oxford: Clarendon, 1933) p.448

[2] H. Mottu, "The Pharisee and the Tax Collector: Sectarian Notions as Applied to the Reading of Scripture" in *Union Seminary Quarterly Review* (1974) p.200

[3] C. Meyers, "Jerusalem Temple" in *The Anchor Bible Dictionary* Vol 6, p.360

[4] See M. Borg, *Conflict, Holiness and Politics in the Teachings of Jesus* (New York: Edwin Mellen, 1984) p.32

[5] A.G. Wright, "The Widow's Mites: Praise or Lament? A Matter of Context" in *Catholic Biblical Quarterly* 44 (1982) p.262

[6] A. Saldarini, *Pharisees, Scribes and Sadducees in Palestinian Society* (Edinburgh: T & T Clark, 1989) p.284

[7] V. Shillington, "A Tale of Two Taxations: The Parable of the Pharisee and the Toll Collector" in V. Shillington (Ed.), *Jesus and his Parables*, p.27

[8] J.R. Donahue, "Tax Collectors and Sinners" in *Catholic Biblical Quarterly* 33 (1971) p.45

[9] N. Perrin, *Rediscovering the Teaching of Jesus*, pp.93-102

[10] K.E. Bailey, *Through Peasant Eyes*, p.153

[11] T.W. Manson, *The Sayings of Jesus*, p.312

[12] B.B. Scott, *Hear Then the Parable*, p.97

[13] See D. McBride, *The Gospel of Mark: a Reflective Commentary* (Dublin: Dominican Publications, 1996) pp.176-181

[14] W.R. Herzog, *Parables as Subversive Speech*, pp.192-193